D1449103

WHAT I TELL YOU THREE TIMES IS TRUE

WHAT
I TELL YOU
THREE TIMES
IS TRUE

□

Jessica Davidson

THE McCALL PUBLISHING COMPANY
New York

*For Judy, who knows better
than to listen more than once*

Contents

☐

WHAT I TELL YOU THREE TIMES IS TRUE

I

Who Are You?

□

Some years ago a reporter walked around the streets of New York City stopping strangers at random. He asked each one, "Who are you?" and wrote down exactly what they said in reply. A few people, of course, were simply annoyed and said something like, "What do you mean who am *I*? Who are you?" or, "What are you, some kind of nut?" But most people gave straightforward answers.

There were a great many different answers, but it is possible to classify them into the following typical groups:

1. I am James McKinley.
2. I am an American (or an Irish-American or an Italian).
3. I am a Jew (or a Catholic or a Methodist).
4. I am a Republican (or a Democrat or a Socialist).
5. I am an electrical engineer (or I'm studying to be a chemist).
6. I am a Boy Scout (or an Elk or a member of the League of Women Voters).

7. I am the oldest of five boys (or the mother of three children).
8. I'm an amateur photographer (or a nature lover or a boxing fan).
9. I'm an easygoing guy who minds his own business (or I'm a poet searching for the meaning of life).
10. I am from Pittsburgh and I'm visiting my cousin in Brooklyn.
11. I'm nobody in particular. Who did you think I was?

The answers show what each speaker thought was most important to reveal about himself. What is it that you would want a stranger to know about you at first meeting? Your name alone? Name, rank, and serial number is that bare minimum of information a captured soldier must give to the enemy. Unless your name is famous or unless it indicates national origin at the very least, it is less revealing of yourself than any other answer you might give. On the other hand, it is the one kind of answer that enables the stranger to identify you as exactly the person you are. When you answer "Who are you?" with your name alone, you are saying two things: (1) I want you to know who I am, me, an individual, not just one of a number of members of some vaguely defined group; and (2) my name is all you need to know about me on first meeting, I'm not about to spread my life out before a stranger.

If you answered the question by giving your national origin, your religion, your political party, your club membership or your occupation, it is fair to conclude that you want to be known as a member of one of these groups, that membership is of great importance to you and perhaps you would like to be regarded as a spokesman for the group. If the reporter was trying to find out how Irish-Americans or Republicans feel about the space program, you could tell him.

The other types of answers, except the last, are the answers of people willing to be known, telling about themselves what they think will most interest a stranger, so that the conversation will continue. The last type of answer, "I'm nobody in particular," is the answer of a person who thinks so little of himself that he is convinced he's being spoken to only because he's been mistaken for someone else.

Each of these answers holds up a mirror to the speaker's face and shows, to some small degree, how he views himself. What do you see when you look into the mirror? A good-looking, intelligent, self-possessed individual or a sad sack? And what does it matter?

If a girl is twelve, does it matter whether she thinks of herself as a baby or a child or almost a teen-ager? If a woman is sixty, does it matter whether she sees herself simply as an adult or as an old woman? Will her self-portrait affect her clothes, her mannerisms, her activities and interests in each of these cases?

Do you do better on tests, or in contests, if you see yourself as an easy winner or a sure loser?

These questions have obvious answers, but others less obvious follow the same pattern. If you feel the part, you will look the part. And if you look the part, you may be given it. But there's another side to the question. No matter what you answer to the question "Who are you?" you set off some kind of reaction in the mind of your questioner.

"Clarence? Your name is Clarence! People named Clarence are sissies." Really? Was your character determined for life because your parents decided on a name for you when you were no more than hours old? Would your life have been entirely different if they had named you James? Yes, in a sense, it would, because as James you would never have to defend yourself against this particular form of prejudgment. Many boys named Clarence or Wilbur or Floyd or Francis introduce themselves as Chuck or Will or Skip or Frank to get them over that first hurdle. But you can't get over all such hurdles. Whatever your name, your new acquaintance has *some* built-in association, favorable or unfavorable, which will shape his reaction to the sound of your name. When Bobby Kennedy was campaigning for the presidency, did he help or hurt his chances by being "Bobby" rather than "Robert"?

Surnames often arouse more prejudgments than first names. Suppose a job is advertised in a newspaper. There's a box number to which written replies may be sent. A hundred answers come in. How many letters will be tossed unread into the wastebasket because of the signature alone? "Tom Wang," the employer reads and says to himself, "No. Orientals are sneaky. Carlos Sanchez? Probably a Mexican. Mexicans are lazy. Gino Scarlatti? An Italian fellow who worked for me once was a careless and sloppy worker. Adam Polonski? No. Poles are too stupid. Timothy O'Connor? The Irish drink too much. I won't take a chance. David Epstein? Jews are pushy. He'll try to take my customers away from me and start his own competing business. Ah, here's a good one! William Robinson. Let's see what his qualifications are." Of course William Robinson isn't going to get the job on the basis of his name alone, but his letter will be read and considered while the others' letters will not be.

This is what is meant by prejudice: a decision made for or against, but usually against, someone or something without sufficient basis. The employer who reacts by tossing away the letters because of the names of the applicants is showing his prejudices against people on the basis of their national origin alone.

Are all advance judgments prejudices? What *is* a sufficient basis for a decision? Many people will tell you they're not prejudiced, that their opinions are based on experience. "When you've seen one, you've seen them all," they say, and thus condemn any number of people they've never met.

When you've seen one, you've seen them all. Well, perhaps. If you've been bitten by a mosquito and are thereafter unwilling to let another mosquito settle on your arm, nobody's going to accuse you of prejudice. But suppose you've been bitten once by a dog?

Let's take it a little further: There's a boy named Joe who has black hair, is left-handed, wears glasses, is an excellent soccer player, collects coins as a hobby and plays trumpet in the school band. You and Joe were friends and shared a locker at school. One day when you couldn't find a pen you were sure you had left in the locker, you asked Joe if he'd taken it. He thought he was being accused of stealing and became very angry. He retaliated against the supposed insult by accusing you, in front of your friends and one of your teachers, of being a liar and a cheat. Because of the lies he told about you, you got into a lot of trouble. The quarrel was never made up. You and Joe are no longer friends.

Do you conclude from this experience that black-haired people are quick-tempered? That left-handed people are sneaky? That nobody who wears eyeglasses can be trusted? That soccer players or coin collectors or trumpet players are no-good, mean, touchy, backsliding, vindictive, vengeful people? Not likely.

And if it happens that Joe is a Negro, or a Mexican, or a . . . are you in any better position to say that Negroes or Mexicans are untrustworthy than to say that coin collectors are? And if not, just what is the value of the experience that is said to back up the prejudgment, "When you've seen one, you've seen them all."? One *what*? One guy named Joe. You don't like him. You're justified. What about other guys named Joe? Well, what about them?

Prejudices are highly contagious. Many people who have never even seen a Jew are sure they don't like Jews. They believe what other prejudiced people have told them. For many people in many circumstances the label alone is enough. They do not look for proof nor wait to have it shown to them. They know they don't like Negroes or Japanese or Germans or Puerto Ricans and, because they know this with such certainty in advance, they never allow themselves the opportunity to find out whether there is a particular Negro or Japanese or German or Puerto Rican who might become their close friend.

According to an old story, a man had a faithful dog who had been with him for many years. When the dog was old and losing his teeth and needing extra care, the man was tired of him. But he could not bring himself to kill his dog Tray who had once been such a faithful companion. So he turned the animal into the streets with the cry of "Mad dog! mad dog!" and then someone else killed poor Tray.

In just this way young children pick up the words and phrases adults use to show their prejudices. They do not yet understand what the words mean nor even against whom they are to be directed, but they know that the words show hate and anger and they use them for this purpose. Listen to six-year-olds calling each other names. "You're a dirty nigger!" "You're nothing but shanty-Irish!" "You're a spic!" "You're a wop!" "You're a dumb Polack!" If this is what you hear, you know a great deal about the prejudices of the parents of these children. You know nothing about the children except that they are angry. The "nigger" may be Chinese, the "Polack" may be French-Canadian.

"Sticks and stones may break my bones but words will never hurt me." It's a good phrase to shout back at your name callers, but it's far from true. The names people call you may affect not only other people's view of you but also your view of yourself. If they hold up a distorted mirror before you, your picture of yourself will be distorted. Does your work at school improve if your classmates continually tell you how dumb you are? Are you more apt to catch that high fly if someone yells, "Hey, clumsy, let's see you drop it!"?

Official actions that place you in a group already labeled are even harder to withstand. Do members of the "low" reading group feel the same way about themselves as members of the "top" reading group? But at least your placement in the "low" or "top" group was in some way connected with your school performance up to the time of your placement there. Suppose people's high or low opinion of you had nothing to do with who you were as a person or with anything you had ever done or failed to do. Suppose you heard it said again and again that you were lazy, stupid, dirty, sneaky, and dangerous with knives, and suppose that not only had you done nothing to deserve this opinion but also there was nothing you could do to change it because your skin happened to be black and you lived in a community of people who held these prejudices against Negroes. Suppose that every ambition you had was stopped cold because the jobs you wanted were not open to you, because you did not belong, were not wanted. Is it possible that, whoever you were to start with, you might become somewhat lazy, stupid, dirty, sneaky, and dangerous with knives? At the very least, you are likely to become defensive and wary of each new person you meet. How can you know whether or not he holds these prejudices? Perhaps you are about to be hit, verbally, again. Have you reached out a hand to pat a strange dog only to find him shrink away from you as if he expects to be hit? And if he does not shrink away but snarls instead because he expects to be hit, can you blame him if, in his experience, he has been more often beaten than patted?

Labels have an extraordinary effect on the persons labeled and on those who use the label to classify them. Does a janitor feel more dignified if he's called "custodian" or "building superintendent"? Is garbage collecting a better job if the garbageman has the title of "sanitary engineer"? Yes, because words, in the way we use them, seem to have a force of their own.

An interesting experiment was tried a few years ago in a California school. It was an attempt to find out whether a teacher's opinion of a pupil's intelligence had any effect on the pupil's progress. The idea for this experiment came to Robert Rosenthal's mind as a result of some experiments he had already done with laboratory rats. It was the laboratory assistants, as well as the rats, who were the subject of his experiments. He told the laboratory assistants that the rats they were to train had been specially bred for their intelligence, though this was not true. Remarkably, the rats performed far better than average in finding their way through the mazes. At the same time another group of rats, in no way different from the first group, performed poorly, far below average, in the hands of laboratory assistants who had been told the animals were especially dull.

With this experience behind him, Mr. Rosenthal was ready for his school experiment. He told a group of teachers that the children in their classes would make tremendous progress in their schoolwork during the coming year because they were a specially selected group of bright children. The prediction was correct. The children made spectacular progress although, in fact, they were a normal class with average I.Q.

Perhaps, as the old proverb would have it, "you can't make a silk purse out of a sow's ear." The trick is to call it a silk purse and the chances are that nobody will investigate what it's made of.

Prejudices based on names and labels alone are not confined to the names of people.

> *What's in a name? That which we call a rose*
> *By any other name would smell as sweet.*

Not by a long shot. The way you react to smells and tastes and sounds of people and things, particularly the first time you encounter something new, is determined to a far greater degree than you might imagine by the name of the new thing or its label. Of course, there are limits. You can probably remember being led into swallowing some rather bad-tasting medicine by your mother's assurance of "Taste it. It's good." So you tasted it and then you spat it out. No matter what you call castor oil, it's still going to be a pretty messy business. And probably no matter what you call a rose, it will smell sweet. But consider some of the in-between tastes and smells. Consider particularly the things people have to "develop a taste for." Almost no one likes the taste of beer or whiskey or cigarettes on the first try. If these were labeled medicine, nobody would try them twice of his own free will. But they're supposed to be something special, they're promoted by the advertisers with such glowing words as "rich" and "mellow," and so people go on drinking or smoking until they get used to it.

Advertising agencies spend a great deal of time and effort just thinking up names for products that will arouse favorable prejudices. Do Tang or Wink sound like something good to drink? Think of Jaguars and Cougars and Mustangs, Barracudas and Thunderbirds. What is it that drivers would like a car to do? And is the name a guarantee that the car will do it? A rose called stinkweed will smell the same, but Stinkweed Perfume just won't sell as well as Essence of Roses.

II

What's Your Right Name?

☐

In France, they call a horse "*cheval*" and in Germany, they call it "*pferd*," but of course the right name for a horse is "horse." Don't you agree?

In the minds of very young children, a name belongs to the thing that is named and is as much a part of it as its size, shape, color, and function. Pigs are called pigs because they're so dirty. The sun is called the sun because it shines. It couldn't be called anything else because its name is the sun. It would not have been possible to call the sun "moon" and the moon "sun," a child told the psychologist Jean Piaget, who was investigating children's understanding of the world, because the sun is brighter than the moon. The right name for the sun is "sun." If you called it anything else, you would just be wrong.

The adult version of this is "Let's call a spade a spade." In a memorandum to the Foreign Office, Winston Churchill wrote:

I do not consider that names that have been familiar for generations in England should be altered to study the whims of foreigners living in those parts. Where the name has no particular significance the local custom should be followed. However, Constantinople should never be abandoned, though for stupid people Istanbul may be written in brackets after it. As for Angora, long familiar with us through the Angora cats, I will resist to the utmost of my power its degradation to Ankara. . . . If we do not make a stand we shall in a few weeks be asked to call Leghorn Livorno, and the B.B.C. [British Broadcasting Corporation] will be pronouncing Paris "Paree."

Well, what *is* the right name for Paris? Does the right name for Berlin rhyme with Merlin, or is it Bare-leén? Who is right, the people of the state of Arkansas (ár-can-saw) or the people of the state of Missouri who live along the banks of the Arkansas (ar-cán-zas) River? And who decides?

If you think these questions are unanswerable, you're probably right, but if you think they're silly, watch out. A great part of your life may be affected by other people's belief that the name of the thing is of great importance, that perhaps it is even the thing itself.

Some people who are out of work through no fault of their own are too proud to accept charity. They would rather starve. They will not go "on relief" and they will not apply for "welfare." Community opinion supports them, having in general a poor opinion of people who are "on welfare." They are thought to be getting something for nothing at the expense of hard-working people who have to pay high taxes to support the loafers. But there's nothing wrong with living on "Social Security" payments or with collecting "Unemployment Insurance." Where does the money come from to pay Social Security and Unemployment Insurance? It's not the charity itself that a person with pride cannot allow himself to accept. It's the word "charity." What is the "right name" for help to the unemployed?

People who are superstitious believe that the number 13 brings bad luck. This is silly enough in itself, but it's possible to be sillier and to hold that it's not only the number 13 that's unlucky but even the name of the number. Take a ride in an elevator of any of a large number of apartment buildings in New York City and watch the numbers of the floors as you pass them. Here comes 10, then 11, then 12, and here's 14. There was no 13. If you ask the elevator operator, he'll explain that people don't like to rent apartments on the thirteenth floor and that's why the building doesn't have any thirteenth floor.

Some people believe that names have magical powers. To know a man's true name, in some primitive societies, is to have power over him, for his name can be used in curses and spells in much the same way that his fingernail parings or strands of his hair can be stirred into the witch's brew. When the princess found out Rumpelstiltskin's name, she had him in her power. Some Hindu parents whose first child has died will be careful in naming the second to call it by some ugly and belittling name like Trashpile. The hope is that if the child is so unworthy, no one will waste a curse upon it. Eastern European Jewish parents of the last century, in similar circumstances named a child Alter, which means the old one, to fool the devil (who presumably had killed the first child) into thinking that this child was not a child at all. If "Alter" survived to the age of thirteen, the age at which tradition said he became a man, he could then be given his right name.

In all kinds of superstitions the name itself, even its spelling, is of great importance. Numerologists who claim to be able to predict your future by giving a numerical value to the letters of your name will caution you against changing the spelling. If your right name is Catherine and you are so foolhardy as to change it to Kathryn, you may alter the whole course of your life. Like the makers of horoscopes, numerologists will tell you, by adding and manipulating the number values of the letters in your name, whether this is a good day for you to board an airplane or not. They can also tell you, so they claim, whether to sign your full name or just your initials if you're about to take a difficult test or apply for a job. One way you'll succeed, the other you won't. Children play a game of pairing off the letters of their names with those of their friends. After all the matching letters are crossed out in a pair of names, the remaining letters are counted out to the chant of "Love, Marriage, Friendship, Hate." How dreadful when it turns out, as in the example below, that Mary loves Frank but he hates her:

MA~~R~~Y ~~GO~~LDE~~N~~
F~~RAN~~K ~~CI~~R~~O~~

Advise poor Mary! She has only to spell out his "right name," Francis, and it will turn out that he wants to marry her:

MARY GOLDEN
FRANCIS GIRO

This is a children's pastime, but many adults pay serious attention to facts like these: When Lincoln was shot, he was sitting in the Ford theater. When Kennedy was shot, he was sitting in a Lincoln car, made by the Ford company. The vice-president serving under Lincoln was named Johnson. So was the vice-president serving under Kennedy. Lincoln's secretary was named Kennedy. Kennedy's secretary was named Lincoln. The facts are curious. Do you believe they are significant? If so, could Kennedy have avoided assassination by hiring a secretary named Kelly?

If the name of the thing is the thing itself, then perhaps if you don't mention the name the thing will cease to exist. "Speak of the Devil and he'll appear" is a maxim that advises you to avoid even the mention of unpleasantness because, if you do, the misfortune may occur. We have fire insurance which will give us money to build a new house if our house is destroyed by fire. Accident insurance will furnish the money to pay medical bills. And then there's theft insurance. Apparently, it's safe to mention fire and accident and theft. But there's no sickness insurance and there's no death insurance. Instead we have health insurance and life insurance. Do they guarantee health and life?

The term "death" is one we seldom use about present events and people and animals who are close to us. We put an incurably sick pet dog to sleep. We do not put him to death. *Our* relatives do not die; they pass away.

Good magic as well as bad can be worked with words

alone. We have come a long way from the times when "Open Sesame" would roll back a stone door from the mouth of the cave of treasure, when "Abracadabra" could make us rich in an instant. But we have our magic words today, too. The cheerleaders at the ball game don't shout "Abracadabra," but does what they shout have any more meaning or effect on the outcome? In the 1920s a man named Couée started a tremendous fad: All you had to do to improve yourself and to get ahead was to chant each morning when you awoke, "Every day in every way I'm getting better and better."

A prison official in California believed that this trick could be worked electronically. Each prisoner was supplied with an earphone beside his pillow while he slept. A ten-minute tape recording, part of it sounding like a sermon and part of it sounding as though the prisoner were talking to himself, played repeatedly all through the night. This is part of what was on the tape:

> "You will have faith in yourself, faith in others and faith in the essential decency of mankind. You will know your faults and you shall overcome them. You can and will solve life's problems. You are filled with love and compassion for all. You will do this with the help of God. I am filled with love and compassion for all, so help me God.

There is no record to show whether the prisoners who listened to this tape night after night for the years of their jail sentences became model citizens after they were released from prison. Do you suppose this worked? Or don't you believe in magic?

People who prepare television advertising do. They

believe that if the name of a soft drink is flashed on the screen again and again, so quickly that you're hardly aware you've seen it, pretty soon you'll be persuaded to get up and open a can of that drink. Will you?

Even when the name is not thought to be magical in itself, it still assumes an extraordinary importance in the minds of some people. They believe that when they have learned the name of something, they know a great deal about it, perhaps all they need to know. This was all that the employer in the story of the first chapter felt he needed to know about the Mexican who was applying for a job; the mere label was enough.

Have you ever watched how some people look at abstract paintings in an art gallery? They stand for a while and look at a painting, trying to figure out what it "is." Then, with the sort of look on their faces that says "I give up," they move closer to read the title. "Media 12," they read and are satisfied. Now they know what it is and can move on to look at the next one. Some people feel they know all there is to know about birds or flowers or constellations if they have learned to identify them by name. Knowing American history, for such people, is knowing how to recite the names of the presidents in proper order.

If you know the name of something, you know what it "is" and you know how to deal with it. Is an old worn desk "second-hand furniture"? If so, it's inexpensive and may even be given away. Of course if it's "antique," it's worth a lot of money.

In the Greek myth, Procrustes tortured all who came his way by tying them to an iron bed. He demanded that each of his victims fit the bed exactly. If they were too short for the bed, he stretched their legs by force until they were long enough. If they were too tall, he lopped off their legs to the proper length. In much the same way, people often insist that circumstances be made to fit the words they have chosen to describe them. What is an "amateur" athlete in contrast to a "professional"? An amateur doesn't get paid for his work. Do you know some of the roundabout methods that are used to pay huge sums of money to amateur athletes, by way of prizes and college scholarships and so forth? The pay must be given in such a way as not to destroy their "amateur" standing. If they are no longer "amateurs" they are not permitted to compete for the big money prizes.

Judges and lawyers spend a great deal of their working time fitting things and circumstances to the words of the law. The Constitution states that no "person" shall be deprived of life, liberty, or property without due process of law. What absurd results follow from the decision that a corporation like General Motors is a "person"?

The Wage and Hour Law was enacted to make sure that workers would be paid at least a minimum wage for their work and that they would receive overtime pay in addition if they worked long hours. In enforcing the law it was found that in some industries housewives were working at home for very low wages. As they were paid for the pieces they produced rather than by the hour, it was very difficult to prove what their hourly earnings were. For this reason, homework was absolutely forbidden in certain industries. In other industries where the problem was not so severe, homework was allowed provided certain records were kept. One of the industries in which homework was forbidden was the embroidery industry. If a housewife edged a sleeve with two or three rows of crocheting, she was violating the law. But if she crocheted a whole cuff to be added to the sleeve, she was not violating the law, because cuffs were classified as part of the Knitted Outerwear Industry in which homework was permitted. How many rows of crocheting make a cuff? Grown men spent hours and hours arguing the point.

Under the same law, child labor is generally forbidden. But there are certain exceptions. For example, children are allowed to deliver newspapers. But what is a newspaper? The *Daily News* clearly is. The advertisement for a Sears Roebuck sale, printed on newsprint and folded like a newspaper, clearly isn't. But what of the paper that contains two news articles of local interest in twenty pages of local advertising? Three news articles? Four? And when you have decided the question, what does it have to do with the problem of whether it is a good or a bad thing for children to work after school?

The pancreas is a gland which empties into the intestine. Do you want to eat a pancreas? Does it taste better when it's called a "sweetbread"? Which is its right name?

What a pretty yellow flower! Oh, no, it's just a weed. Who wants a vase full of weeds?

Knowing the "right name" of a thing relieves you from the job of thinking about it. In fact, it may even prevent you from thinking about it. Everybody knows that "acid" is dangerous. That is why, when a jar with the word "acid" on the label broke and spilled its contents on the schoolroom floor, the janitor was especially careful not to touch the mop to wring it out and not to let the liquid touch his shoes. The spilled liquid happened to be vinegar. Was "vinegar" its right name, or was its right name "acetic acid"?

A teacher gave a class the problem of finding the surface area of the 2-inch molding used to make a picture frame around a picture whose dimensions were 24 by 36 inches. The right name for the shape of each of the pieces of molding is "trapezoid," so of course, the problem involved computing the area of two sets of equal trapezoids.

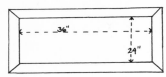

If you forget about the "right name" of each piece of molding can you see an easier way to find the total area of the frame?

Then too, there is the problem of whether, when the right name of a thing has been learned and the thing has therefore been properly classified, it is guaranteed to remain the same. Is the child who was rightly named "slow learner" in the first grade still a slow learner? Are you exactly the same person you were when you were in first grade? Do all the "right names" that were applied to you then still apply? By placing a caterpillar in an escape-proof cage, can you prevent its becoming a moth? Is a "right name" sometimes a cage like this?

Perhaps we should take more seriously the old riddle Lincoln is said to have asked:

"If you call a tail a leg, how many legs does a dog have?" The answer is four, because calling a tail a leg doesn't make it one.

III

The Camera Doesn't Lie

EXHIBIT 1

Hans Jedermann is on trial. He is accused of having stolen a valuable painting from a house on Main Street on the morning of March 19. A witness against him states under oath that she was sitting at the window of the ground-floor living room of the house across the street and that at 10 A.M. on March 19, she saw Hans Jedermann enter number 23 Main Street by the side door. Ten minutes later, she says, she saw him leave by the same door, carrying a bulky package.

Hans Jedermann's lawyer produces a photo of number 23 Main Street, taken from across the street. He shows it to the jury as Exhibit 1 to convince them that the witness is lying because she could not possibly have seen Hans enter or leave by the side door through that thick hedge.

The district attorney protests that the picture is not true. He requests a recess in which to go to the scene of the crime and take his own photograph. The recess is granted. An hour later the district attorney returns with a photo that *he* took from across the street. It is received by the court as Exhibit 2.

EXHIBIT 2

During the same recess, a news photographer, realizing that the height of the hedge was going to be an important point in the trial, went to the scene on his own and took the photo labeled Exhibit 3, also from across the street. Fortunately, he also took along a tape measure and so was able to report the following facts: The height of the hedge was four feet. The window at which the witness said she sat was three feet from the ground.

EXHIBIT 3

Which of the three is a "true" picture?

In one sense, they are all "true" pictures. They are all photographs of number 23 Main Street, taken from across the street, as the photographers said. Nobody lied about this, and certainly the camera doesn't lie, as everyone knows. But only Exhibit 3 is the "true" picture for the purpose for which it was shown to the jury. To get the Exhibit 1 photo, the camera was placed on the sidewalk. Exhibit 2 was taken from the roof of the house across the street. Exhibit 3 was taken by the news reporter who stood on the sidewalk across the street and held the camera against his chest, at just about the level of the eyes of someone who might be sitting at the window of the house behind him.

The camera doesn't lie. It reports accurately what can be seen from the viewpoint at which it is placed. Every report, whether it is made in pictures or in words, is made from some viewpoint. It helps to know what that viewpoint is in deciding whether or not to accept the report as truth.

In court, witnesses are asked to swear to tell "the truth, the whole truth, and nothing but the truth." A witness can fulfill his pledge to tell the truth and nothing but the truth, from his viewpoint, but he cannot possibly tell the "whole truth." If he could, no one would have the patience to listen. Try, for example, to tell the whole truth about what you are doing at this moment. It is simply not enough to say that you are reading this book. Are you sitting or lying down? How are you sitting? Are your legs crossed? How are you holding the book? Did you turn the page with your right hand or your left? In what surroundings are you reading? Are you alone in the room? What sort of light are you reading by? What are you doing besides reading? Are you breathing? What is your pulse rate? Are you digesting a recent meal? Is it absolutely silent where you are? If not, what sounds do you hear? If you heard a sound, did it trigger some thought unconnected with what you are reading? Have your eyes wandered at all from the page to notice anything in the room or outside it?

Enough of this. The point has surely been made. Any report must be selective in what facts it chooses to mention. Any report must therefore leave out some part of the "whole truth."

Consider the following report, an imaginary one, made by Carlos Cadauno, a Spanish boy who lives in a tiny village in the southern part of Spain. Until yesterday, he had never been more than ten miles from his native village. Yesterday he flew to the United States. At the end of his first day of sightseeing, this is part of the letter Carlos wrote home:

I have heard that they do not allow bullfighting in the United States because they think it is too cruel and bloody, but I think they just do not understand bullfighting, because they certainly have their own forms of bloody combat for entertainment here. Today I witnessed a sports contest attended by thousands and thousands of people. Everybody sat on raised benches watching what went on below them in a large field. At the start of the contest, two men stood facing each other. From the way the crowd reacted, it was clear that these two were on opposing sides. One stood with his feet apart, head slightly lowered, with both hands grasping a large, heavy wooden club. He seemed to be threatening to swing this club at the other man who stood about seventy feet from him. He tested the weight of the club and even pounded it against the ground once or twice as if to make sure it could deliver a death-dealing blow. Meanwhile the other man held what seemed to be very smooth white rock. It was clear that he was preparing to throw this rock at the man with the club, and he swung his arm round and round in a threatening manner, as if to gain speed and momentum for the throw. There were quite a few other men on the field, spaced out at intervals but, while they were all watching the two opponents, they did nothing to interfere.

I thought at first that the contest was to see who

could kill the other first, whether the man with the rock could hit the man with the club before he had a chance to advance and club the rock thrower. But now I am not sure that that is the way the contest goes. The man with the rock threw it. The man with the club did not duck, as I had expected him to, but attempted to ward off the rock by striking it with the club. To my astonishment, he succeeded in doing this. The rock went flying off toward one of the bystanders on the field. As soon as he saw what he had done, the man with the club was apparently afraid. He hastily dropped the club and started running.

The bystander, toward whom the rock was traveling at great speed, bravely attempted to catch it so it would not injure others, but he did not succeed. Fortunately, no one was hit. The rock fell to the ground. It was immediately scooped up by one of the bystanders in the field, apparently an accomplice of the rock thrower. This man too tried to hit the clubwielder by throwing the rock in his direction, or perhaps he was trying to throw the rock to another accomplice closer to the runner. I am not sure. In any case, nobody succeeded in hitting the runner. It looked as though the runner was going to be able to get clear off the field before anyone could stop him but, for reasons I never understood, he suddenly stopped running and slid along the ground toward a white sack. The crowd yelled "Safe!" and I guess he was safe, because thereafter nobody tried to throw the rock at him. Instead, a new man came up with a club and the contest started over.

It is true that in all the time I watched, nobody

was clubbed to death or hit with the rock, but I think that this was because the particular contestants I happened to be watching were not very good at this form of combat. I have seen some poor bull-fighters and some cowardly bulls in our own country, so I am not trying to be critical. I'm just reporting the facts.

Carlos reported the facts as he saw them. What is wrong with his report? Certainly not the viewpoint. You might have been sitting next to him at the Series game and have seen exactly what he saw, but it's not likely that your report would sound like his.

Perhaps it helps to know something of the rules of the game, of the reasons for what seem to be meaningless actions? Does the traveler who spends a week in a foreign country and comes home to report on the conditions prevailing there, the opinions of the people about their government and about world affairs, how poor or wealthy they are, and so on, face some of the problems Carlos faced? Are their reports "true"?

Let's come closer to home, to more familiar scenes and to witnesses more like yourself. Here is a report by an outside observer, an adult visitor, of what went on in a sixth-grade classroom from 11:15 A.M. to 12 noon one Tuesday morning. Unlike Carlos, this observer makes no attempt to explain why anyone is doing what he observes. The report is entirely factual and the facts are "true":

Twenty-five children in the classroom, one teacher.

Noise level high. People moving around a great deal, talking to each other and handing objects to each other. Some pupils sitting on the floor, others near them bouncing balls. Some pupils used up a skein of twine, tying short pieces to a desk leg and pulling on the twine to break it. They threw away the pieces. No books were in evidence. Some pupils were scribbling numbers on scraps of paper or on the blackboard. Occasionally they added these numbers and divided the totals, but they did not hand in their work nor consult the teacher. Throughout the period the teacher was simply present. She did not interfere with anything the children were doing nor criticize any behavior.

What do you think was going on?

Would the report have been improved if the observer had glanced briefly at the teacher's lesson plan? It said:

> Session on precision in measurement; identify range and mean. Team work measuring and calculating the mean height a ball bounces and the force required to break eight-pound-test twine.

To report an event meaningfully, you have to know something of what you are looking for. To judge the value of a report made by someone else, you have to know what he understood of what he saw and what it was he was looking for. Of course, this does not mean that you cannot find something if you're not looking for it. The Persian fairy tale *The Three Princes of Serendip* gave rise to the word serendipity, the art of finding valuable or pleasant things without looking for them. You may find a pearl on the beach when you are looking only for attractive pebbles or shells, but you will not find the pearl if you go to the beach simply to swim.

What do you see when you look at this picture? A man making a speech to a crowd? or Lincoln delivering the Gettysburg address? That depends, doesn't it, on whether you recognize a picture of Lincoln.

Even when two people look at an event with exactly

the same amount of background knowledge and even if they choose exactly the same facts to report, their choices of words to describe these facts may differ so greatly, because of their bias, that the reports may not be alike at all.

How would you headline a sports story about a ball game in which the Green Sox won over the Blue Jays by a score of 4-2? These are some of the possibilities:

SOX CRUSH JAYS 4-2

SOX EDGE JAYS BY TWO POINTS

SOX STOP JAYS 4-2

SOX TROUNCE JAYS, DOUBLE JAYS' SCORE

SOX ROUT JAYS

JAYS SNATCH ONLY 2, SOX TRIUMPH

Suppose someone is describing Jennifer Smith, who is five feet three inches tall and weighs ninety-five pounds. Does he say she is skinny? slim? slender? willowy? a stringbean of a girl? Can you tell by his choice of words whether he thinks Jennifer is pretty? whether he is biased in favor of Jennifer or against her?

Is the old man who's been putting his money in the savings bank thrifty or stingy? And if, instead, he bought stock, would he be investing or gambling? In the larger community, would you describe the activity as hoarding or stockpiling? Considering the Songmy incident in the Vietnam war, how far away from your target must you be before murder of civilians turns into heroic successful attack? Is murder by napalm from aircraft more moral than ground-level murder?

If the selection of facts to report is made in such a way as to favor a particular point of view or to lead to a particular conclusion, the report is biased, or slanted, toward one side of an argument. A reporter may be aware of his bias or not, but the listener can discover the bias if he listens carefully. Someone is caught stealing the plans for a nuclear submarine. Is he a "spy" or an "intelligence officer"? It depends whose side he's on, the reporter's side or the side of the reporter's enemy. During a war the army "executed a strategic withdrawal" or "retired to a new position commanding a better view of the terrain" if the army that was moving back of its front line was the reporter's army. If it was the enemy's army, then it "retreated" or "was routed" or was at least "driven back."

All of the words in quotation marks in the last paragraph are *color* words, intended not merely to report an event but also to influence the reader's opinion about that event. They show the bias of the reporter, whether he is aware of it or not.

If all biased reports could be recognized as such by the color words used in them, it would be easy to discover the bias and to discount it in search of "the truth." But what is *not* reported is often as significant in showing bias as the words that are used. The trouble is, it's not always easy to spot what's been left out. Even a camera whose lens covers the entire scene is still selecting some part of the "whole truth." Where in the picture is the main point of clear focus? Other objects, nearer or farther from the lens, will be somewhat blurry. How does the perspective change the apparent size of the objects photographed? (Have you seen photos in which a man's foot appears to be twice the size of his head?) From which angle was the photo taken? What is behind the building in the foreground? What is true of the camera is even truer of the reporter who uses words and he, besides, is selecting, out of the many things he saw, just which ones he chooses to describe.

The unbiased reporter is a creature something like a

unicorn or a perfect circle. That is to say, he can be imagined and described but he does not exist. Some reporters are more biased than others but nobody reports an event without *some* bias and nobody could.

Besides, the more unbiased a reporter is, the duller is his report. Let's take a look at what might pass for an unbiased report:

> Henry Makespeech, a state senator from Mission Falls, addressed a meeting of about 250 persons last night in the Mission Falls town hall on the subject "What Are They Teaching Your Children?"

Let's suppose that this is a correct account, and let's also suppose that you've never heard of Mission Falls. What important facts has the reporter left out? Can you tell from the report whether the meeting was well attended? To do so, you'd have to know, at the very least, what the population of Mission Falls is, and you might want to ask some other questions to help you decide.

The report might be rewritten in this way to include the answers to some of your questions:

> Henry Makespeech, state senator from Mission Falls, a town of 3,759 people, addressed a meeting of 263 persons last night in the new town hall meeting room, built to seat 1,500. His subject was "What Are They Teaching Your Children?"

The report is still perfectly accurate, and there is not a single color word in it, but are you beginning to feel that perhaps Senator Makespeech isn't very popular? Well, yes, you might say, but that's not the reporter's

fault. He's only telling the facts. Sure. But which facts?
Let's add a few and see if the picture changes:

> Last night, at the height of the storm that left the
> little town of Mission Falls (population 3,759)
> knee-deep in snow, more than half of all the mothers
> of elementary school-age children in the town braved
> their way through the blizzard to a special PTA
> meeting at the town hall and paid an admission price
> of $1 to hear an address by Senator Henry Make-
> speech on the subject "What Are They Teaching
> Your Children?" Average attendance at PTA meet-
> ings is only about 50, and when Councilman John
> Chilliwether, contender for the state senate seat next
> fall, addressed an open PTA meeting last month he
> mustered a crowd of 75. Thus Mrs. George
> Manager, PTA president, was understandably
> elated over last night's turnout of 263 in the new
> meeting room of the town hall. Senator Make-
> speech's address, which stressed the need for up-
> dating courses in science and social studies, was
> enthusiastically received by the audience, and the
> question-and-answer period extended the meeting
> far beyond its announced closing time of 10 P.M.

This last version of the report contains a great many
color words, intended to influence your feelings: "knee-
deep in snow," "braved," "elated," "enthusiastically received." Obviously this is a slanted report, biased in favor
of Senator Makespeech. But, assuming that it really was
snowing, that everyone who attended had to pay an admission fee, that the meeting was open only to parents
of school-age children, and that the other facts are true

as stated, which report gives a clearer picture of the event? What is the effect of telling, in the second version of the report, that the meeting hall seats 1,500? What is the effect, in the third version, of mentioning the attendance at other PTA meetings and at the meeting at which Senator Makespeech's opponent spoke? Is the choice of these facts as influential as the use of any color words might be?

Quite often the reporter is unaware of his bias and may even deny that he has one. If you are very sure of the correctness of your own viewpoint, you may really believe that no other point of view can possibly be held by intelligent people. Those who disagree with you are, in your opinion, either too stupid to understand the situation or too lazy to get the facts. If they knew the facts and understood them, they would agree with you. Sometimes you can be so sure of this that you take for granted, without asking, that they do agree with you, thus "projecting" your point of view upon them. Here are two examples of such projection:

The streetcar company in a town had installed a speaker system in all the streetcars through which music programs could be heard by the riders. Letters poured into the offices of the streetcar company, both for and against the music. These two were typical:

Dear Sirs:

Congratulations on the new service you have provided for your riders. The music is a great help to us who have a long, boring ride to and from work every day. It makes the ride seem so much shorter. I have heard that there are some people who object, but I certainly don't know any who do. Everyone on

the cars I ride seems very pleased to have the music.
If there are any objectors, they're probably just a few
cranks, the kind of people who just can't stand to
see anyone enjoy life. If they don't like the music,
what's to stop them from taking taxis?

Keep up the good work!

Gratefully yours,

A Faithful Rider

Dear Sirs:

May I add my voice to the many thousands you
must already have heard from against your new program of music in the streetcars? Are we not
bombarded by enough noise on all sides in this city,
day and night, without adding any further to the
assault on our ears? Even if the riders enjoyed the
music you play—and what idiots can really enjoy
this meaningless mish-mash of romantic semi-
classical dinner music?—we wouldn't want to hear
it above and under and through the noises of traffic.

Until last week, streetcar rides were pleasant be-
ginnings and endings to the working day, times for
conversation with fellow passengers or for quiet
reading of the newspapers. Now conversations are
drowned out by the blare of the music. The distrac-
tion makes it impossible to read.

If there are fools who really can't do without
some background music every minute of their wak-
ing lives, let them plug in the earphones of their
pocket transistor radios and leave the vast majority
of riders in peace.

Disgusted Rider

From these two letters, it is obvious that there are two sides to the question of whether music on streetcars is desirable. One of the letters may seem much more sensible to you than the other. If it does, the chances are that that's the one you agree with. The point to notice, however, is that each of the letter writers takes it for granted that most people are on his side of the argument. Both deny that there is any "other side" to the question or, if there is, both feel that only cranks or stupid fools support it. Each writer projects his feelings on everyone else.

In every presidential election emotions run high. Many Democrats are unable to understand the possibility that any normally intelligent person could be a Republican. Many Republicans believe that only uneducated, gullible people claim to be Democrats.

If you have ambitions to be a news reporter, why not try your hand at writing a news article for a Boston paper of December, 1773, describing the Boston Tea Party. When you're finished to your satisfaction, try writing the article for the London paper of the same date.

The situation is complicated enough when there are just two sides to a question. But questions are often three-sided, four-sided, hexagonal. From how many different angles can you photograph a scene? Each viewpoint will present a slightly different picture.

Take any atlas you can find in your classroom or library. Open it to a map of the world. Where do you find the mainland of the United States on it? Is it all in one unbroken piece near the center? What happens to the Soviet Union? Is one piece of it on the far left and the other on the far right? Does the Soviet Union really come apart in the middle? If your atlas contains a polar map, which hemisphere appears in "normal" position, the western or the eastern? Turn the page around so that Florida is toward the top of the page. Does the map look upside down? Is it?

What is a foreigner? If you went to Sweden, would you be a foreigner? Do they have some odd customs in foreign countries? Is the United States a foreign country?

IV

What I Tell You Three Times Is True

☐

I have here, ladies and gentlemen, an object of art that everyone wants to own. It is the very symbol of our national pride, including, as it does, a finely detailed portrait, etched in metal, of one of our greatest and most beloved heroes and containing a touching statement of our deep religious faith as well. Precision-made of highly polished metal, beautifully constructed and flawless in workmanship, it is indeed a little treasure.

I myself have long been the proud possessor of similar objects of art, and not a day goes by in which I do not handle one of them and show it to others. I count him poor indeed who does not possess a single one of these. Their value is recognized everywhere in the civilized world.

Ladies and gentlemen, what am I offered? Who will start the bidding? One dollar? Do I hear one dollar?

Will the auctioneer persuade you to bid on his shiny new penny? Look back at his sales pitch. Has he told a single lie?

That all depends on what you mean by a lie.

Is a lie a misstatement of fact? If you say $7 \times 9 = 64$, is that a lie? If you say, "I have a million things to do this morning," is that a lie? It certainly is a misstatement of fact that $7 \times 9 = 64$, but you haven't told a lie when you said it was. The number of things you have to do this morning is probably closer to ten than to a million but that wasn't a lie either. A lie is not just a misstatement of fact. To tell a lie is to tell something you know to be untrue *in order to deceive someone.* Mistakes of fact are not lies and exaggerations which are so huge that nobody would be deceived are not lies either.

On the other hand, it's perfectly possible to tell a lie without making a single false statement. Consider the following conversation:

JOHN: Did you know that Sue's eloped?
MARY: Sue's eloped! Where did you hear that?!

Mary hasn't said she didn't know Sue had eloped, but she has certainly given John the impression that she not only didn't know it but even that she's unwilling to believe it. If, in fact, Mary knew all along that Sue had eloped, was her answer to John a lie?

Getting an idea across without actually saying anything that someone can point to as a lie is quite popular in advertising. There are penalties for making false statements about products so the ad writers have to be very careful not to write anything which can be labeled a deliberate misstatement of fact. What does the following ad really *say*? What is it designed to make you *think* it says?

If you're tired and rundown, it may be because of a lack of iron in your blood. If so, what you need to perk you up is Irontone. Of course, Irontone won't help *everybody* who's feeling tired and rundown. But if you're one of those *special* people whose tiredness is caused by a lack of iron in your blood, Irontone will pep you up. Irontone isn't for everybody, but maybe it's for that special person— you. Won't you give it a try?

Sometimes lies are accomplished by telling a very small portion of the truth and giving the impression either that what you have told is the whole truth or that, at least, it's a fair, representative sample. The review of a movie in the *Daily Telegraph* may have said:

You may not think this is the funniest film ever made, but it will give you one or two hearty laughs.

Suppose the advertisement for the movie quotes the review this way:

. . . funniest film ever made . . . hearty laughs
—*Daily Telegraph*

Suppose the ad writer justifies his quote by saying, "Well, you wouldn't expect me to put the whole review in an ad. I just took out the important words and put in the dots to show that other words had been omitted." Would you believe that the ad writer wasn't aware of selecting just the words he wanted to promote the movie? Was his an honest selection?

But if the ad writer is lying when he says he quoted the *Daily Telegraph* review of the movie, where, exactly, is the lie? Where was the auctioneer's lie in his speech about the penny? Is it possible to lie without saying a single word? The teacher asks Harold where his homework is. Harold, who hasn't done his homework, opens his briefcase and starts fumbling through a bunch of papers. Is he lying?

All of these techniques are used in propaganda, which is the spreading of ideas, information, or rumors for the purpose of helping or injuring a cause or a person. In persuading people to adopt a particular viewpoint or to take a particular action that will help him, the propagandist is not concerned with the question of whether it helps or hurts the people he's trying to persuade. The difference between a biased report and a piece of propaganda is not a large one. The biased reporter may or may not know that his bias distorts the picture. Often he is not aware that he has a bias. He simply believes that his point of view is the best possible one, perhaps the only one, from which to view the scene. But the propagandist is well aware of his bias and knows exactly what he's trying to sell. He purposely chooses only those facts that support his cause, or distorts or alters facts for his purpose, or conceals facts that are unfavorable to his argument. If necessary, he invents facts to prove his point. In fact he is willing to lie.

People with strong biases are the willing helpers of the propagandist. Because they are sure their own viewpoint is the only correct one, they are ready to believe the best about anyone who is on their side and to believe nothing but the worst about people who disagree with them. For them, the propagandist becomes a great and reliable authority because they *want* to believe what he tells them.

If the propagandist can convince a few ordinary, honest people of his viewpoint because his "facts" suit their bias, they will spread his propaganda, believing it to be true. An effective propagandist gets all sorts of people to work for him without their even knowing it. The simplest example is three-year-old Sally. Sally's not a very good customer for beer or cigarettes, but she's a great propagandist for them. Sally can sing the television commercials. She knows them and she finds the tunes catchier than those of her nursery school songs. She sings them all day long, and so her mother—who just might be a good customer for beer or cigarettes—gets ten times the dosage of advertising the sponsors have paid for.

What effect does this have? The advertisers believe that it works. Say something often enough and people will come to believe it. The message doesn't even have to make too much sense. *You can take a cigarette out of the country but you can't take the country out of a cigarette.* What does it mean? *This headache remedy contains twice as much of some ingredient that doctors recommend most.* (They don't even tell you that the ingredient they're talking about is aspirin, because then you might just go buy aspirin.) Besides, it's got four ingredients, not just one or two. How many ingredients should a remedy have? The more the merrier? Does it matter what they are? *This toothpaste has a new ingredient, ZP-17.* Are secret ingredients the best of all? It really doesn't matter. What matters is hearing it over and over. As the Bellman said in Lewis Carroll's *The Hunting of the Snark,*

> Just the place for a Snark! I have said it thrice:
> What I tell you three times is true.

Whether what is being sold is toothpaste or a candidate for the presidency of the United States, the repetition of the name, of a catchy slogan, of a point of view (whether it's the *one beer to have* or it's *Nixon's the one*) seems to have a telling effect. What's important is the repetition and the fact that so many people are repeating it.

If enough people repeat a slogan, pretty soon it becomes the fact that "everybody" knows. Many people will be persuaded to do something that "everybody" is doing. They want to be on the winning side, to jump on the bandwagon. What everybody is buying must be the thing to buy. Where everybody goes is where the action is. Children often try this form of persuasion on their parents as well as on each other. They try to convince their parents that "everybody" is allowed to stay up till ten o'clock, that "everybody" goes to camp, that "everybody" has a three-speed bike.

What everybody is thinking must be the thoughts to think. The propagandist knows that if he can persuade you that everybody agrees with him, he has found a very powerful tool for persuasion. It is hard to hold on to a point of view if you believe that everyone disagrees with you.

But before you start believing what "everybody" believes, it might be wise to find out how "everybody" got the information. Does "everybody" sometimes take a position because one or two popular people are for it, or because one or two unpopular people are against it? Have you ever seen this happen in a classroom?

"Harold," the teacher asks, "do you think cobalt is magnetic?"

Harold says yes.

"How many people agree with Harold?" the teacher continues. Nobody raises his hand. "Well, how many people think cobalt is not magnetic?" John's hand goes up. John is team captain. Twenty hands are raised to join John's. The teacher returns to Harold: "Why do you think cobalt is magnetic, Harold?"

Harold *did* have a reason for thinking so, but he's ready to back down. "I don't know," he says. "I guess I was wrong."

Is the team captain necessarily the most knowledgeable student? Is a baseball player the best authority on what cereals are most nourishing for children's breakfasts? Do you really want the advice of a beautiful movie star on the question of where to go when your car's transmission breaks down?

If "everybody" thinks so, it must be the truth. Fifty million Frenchmen can't be wrong, as the saying goes. But not so long ago, fifty million Germans certainly were. Hitler told them what to believe and since "everybody" knew about the superiority of the Aryans, of course it had to be so.

But if you don't believe things just because "everybody" does, how do you decide what to believe? How do you know what you know? How do you know what's true?

Some people say "seeing is believing." This works well enough for some things, but every sunny day you see the sun go down behind the hills or tall buildings in the western sky. Do you believe it does? If you believe, instead, that the earth is moving around the sun, why do you believe it? Has anyone really proved it to you? Could you prove it to yourself? Not if you believe only what you see. Besides, "seeing is believing" is awfully limiting. Are you about to forego all knowledge of history because you can't go backward in time to look at it? Will you refuse to believe the results of all scientific experiments that you can't personally carry out? About how many people are there in the world? Is there any way of finding out without personally counting them? Do you know when and where you were born?

Most of what you know comes from what somebody told you. It's therefore rather important to decide whom to believe, especially since no one is able to tell you "the truth, the whole truth, and nothing but the truth."

One choice you have is to pick an authority you decide to trust—a parent, a teacher, the author of a reference work—and to believe whatever the authority says. This choice is the easiest because, one you've chosen an authority, there's no work for you to do. All you have to do is ask and you'll get an answer. Many people live out their lives in this way. They know what they know because Authority says it's true. Their problems arise only when and if they happen to meet someone who has a different Authority to rely on. The best either of these two can do in an argument is to say something like:

"My father can lick your father."
"Oh, yeah!"

If you can't find it in *The New York Times Index*, it probably didn't happen, says *The New York Times*.

Probably the Moscow newspaper, *Pravda,* has a similar slogan. Indeed the subtlest and most underhanded form of propaganda (because it is the hardest to nail down) is that of absolutely ignoring the existence of a subject or a person. If you look at fashion models in the advertisements and never see one who is short and plump, how can you help but conclude that short plump girls are nothing, just not there, not in the picture at all? Have you ever seen an oriental as the scientist-hero of a TV serial? If you did see one, you'd expect that some hanky-panky of the Dr. Fu-Manchu variety was about to occur. You wouldn't believe that the oriental was really the hero. Yet many of the top American scientists, Nobel prize winners among them, are of oriental background.

It's easy to see the bias against Indians in a TV western. The Indians always lose. But it was not so easy to see the bias against Negroes who, until a year or two ago, just weren't on the screen at all. Does Charlie Brown have any Negro players on his team? What color is Superman? The recent practice of hiring Negro actors and actresses, models, and announcers on television may have an importance far beyond that of equal job opportunity. If the Negro teacher in *Room 222* is an obviously competent and popular teacher, then you are likely to conclude that competent, popular teachers may be Negro. Is this helpful to Negro boys who would like to be teachers when they grow up? Did you know that until Jackie Robinson made his breakthrough into the Big League, it was ridiculous even to think of a Negro ballplayer? Now it is taken for granted that skin color has nothing to do with being a good ballplayer. Just how hard was it for women to become doctors, lawyers, engineers, jockeys? Just how unlikely did it once seem that

there would ever be a male kindergarten teacher? Will
there ever be a woman President of the United States?
An American President of Chinese ancestry?

Authority can lead you astray by what it tells you and
by what it considers unnecessary to tell you. Propaganda
on a large scale works best without competition. When
a government is run by a dictator who controls everything in the country and has the power to kill or jail
anyone who opposes him and to suppress any newspapers
that criticize him or show the falsity of his pronounce-
ments, it is fairly easy for him to convince the public
that he is "the greatest" and that they "never had it so
good." If people do not have enough to eat, it may be
difficult to persuade them that their government is pro-
viding them with all possible luxuries. But at that point,
the propaganda line can shift. People can be told that in
other countries everyone is much worse off than they are.

People in such countries do not have much choice
about what they can know. They have no way of finding
out what lies have been told, what facts have been distorted, what facts have been concealed. You are much
better off. You have a variety of sources of information
—but *who* controls that information? To the extent
that radio and TV and the newspapers are controlled by
a rather small group of people, to the extent that the
government feels justified in concealing classified information and in hiding or lying about military activities to
protect the "national interest," the difference may be
only one of degree. The news is selected for you. So are
your textbooks.

The best you can do is to attempt to discover what
someone is trying to sell you. The court in Hans Jedermann's trial could have discovered the height of the
hedge from *any* one of the three photos if it could find

50

out where the camera was placed to take that photo. If you can discover the bias of your authority, you may be able to scrape the facts out from under that bias. You may be able to question whether the facts you have been told are really the important ones, whether other facts that have been left out would change the picture.

In the Soviet Union, school children who are studying the United States know most about unemployment in the United States, about the history of lynching in the South, about slums in Harlem and Appalachia, about strikes and riots and crime in the streets. They know very little about the good things in the United States. That, of course, is because education is controlled by the Communists and this is the picture of the United States that the Communists wish to present.

How much better informed are you about the Soviet Union? You have heard about the slave labor camps, the denial of religious freedom, the one-party elections, the crowded apartments, the women who work as street sweepers and miners. What else do you know? How open is your mind to anything else? Would you respond in the same way as the children to whom Professor Bronfenbrenner talked?

Why Do the Russians Plant Trees
Along the Road? *

A Question from Psychologist Urie Bronfenbrenner

A few weeks ago I was showing some photographs I had taken in Russia to a class of fifth and sixth graders in an American school. Most of

* Urie Bronfenbrenner, "Why Do the Russians Plant Trees Along the Road?" *Saturday Review*, January 5, 1963.

the children came from middle class faculty and professional families. Among my pictures were a number of shots of roads lined with young trees.

A child's hand went up: "Why do they have trees along the road?"

A bit puzzled, I turned the question back to the class: "Why do you suppose they have trees?"

Another child's hand rose for eager answer: "So that people won't be able to see what's going on beyond the road."

A girl had a different idea, "It's to make work for the prisoners."

I asked why some of *our* roads have trees planted along the side.

"For shade," the children said. "To keep the dust down."

Where did the children get the idea that the Russians have different reasons than we have for planting trees?

Many of the examples of propaganda in this chapter were chosen from advertising. This is the least harmful form of propaganda, first because you are never in any doubt that the advertiser is trying to sell you something, and second because you have to buy *some* kind of toothpaste or shampoo or soap. Propaganda for politics and to influence social behavior is carried out in much the same way but is much more harmful because it is not at all so easy to discover what the propagandist is trying to sell. After all, you don't have to choose among competing prejudices; you can get along without any. You don't have to buy a war.

V

Thought Control

□

"I'm nine, going-on-ten," an American child will say, anxious to be considered more grown-up. He might be happier if Chinese were his native language. In Chinese it would be correct to say, "I'm ten" the day after his ninth birthday, for in Chinese the number you use to tell your age is the number of years for all or part of which you've been alive. This is the same kind of logic we use when we say we're living in the twentieth century though we haven't yet reached the year 2000.

Becoming a teen-ager is a milestone. How old is a teen-ager? In China he's twelve. Maybe it's not very important but it is one example of how the language you happen to speak controls your thinking.

Not all of your thinking is so restricted, of course. Memories often take the form of pictures. Smells and tastes and sounds can be remembered for themselves and can call forth many memories associated with them. Certainly you can think of swimming without thinking of the word "swimming," and you could think of it even if you did not know the word, had never known it.

Nobody doubts that animals have clear memories of the people and places and other animals they've known. Everyone who has a pet has at least one story to tell of how his pet did some rather elaborate scheming to achieve some goal. The cat, remembering that the last time he was placed in a carrier he was taken for a trip to the vet, looks at the carrier you've just brought down from the attic, runs and hides. Your dog, in a perfectly straightforward attempt at communication, brings you his leash and lays it at your feet to announce that he wishes to be taken for a walk. Memory, association, reaction to outside events, communication with others, all are possible without words, either thought or spoken. Yet, a very large part of what we call thinking—all of the reasoning we do about the world—is done with words and cannot be done without them.

That's why it matters a great deal what words you have at hand to think with. Because you need words to think with, you must fit your thoughts into the framework your own particular language provides for you. Some thoughts are easier to think than others because the words are readily available. For example, which is easier to describe (either to yourself or to others), the colors of the American flag or the taste of celery?

Suppose there was no word in your language for the color purple. You could, of course, still look at something purple and describe it. You could say it was different from blue and from red, a sort of reddish-blue or bluish-red. But you might be more likely to decide that a given purple object was closer to blue than to red and call it blue. You don't believe you'd do that? What color is the print on this page? What is the color of most telephones? What color is the sky on a moonless night? What color is the shadow of a tree in bright sunlight? What color is a crow? Is the answer to all of these "black"? List some more examples of black objects you see around you. Now, if you want to translate your answers into the Navajo language, do you think that all you need to know is the Navajo word for black? You'd be wrong. It won't work, because Navajo has two words for black and they're not interchangeable. One is the black of coal and the other is the black of darkness. To translate, you're going to have to go back and look at your list again. Of course, once you look at examples of blackness with this in mind, you will be able to decide which Navajo "black" to use, but did you see any real difference between them when the one English word "black" was all you had or thought you needed to have?

You might like to try this experiment. Make a collection of spools of thread or small pieces of cloth or buttons, some red, some brown, and the rest in a variety of shades of blue and green. Show your collection to someone and ask him to classify the items by putting them in piles according to their color. Don't tell him how many piles to set up. Watch what happens. When he's done, ask him to tell you how he's grouped them. Try this with several different people. Choose at least one very young child, one about kindergarten age, one about eight years old, someone your own age, and at least one adult. If you know an artist, be sure to include him. And don't neglect your own classification. Is there any connection between the classifications people make and their knowledge of the names of colors? Did your kindergarten or preschool child put all the greens together or did he separate out the aqua, the chartreuse, the olive green? Did he make separate piles of robin's egg blue, navy blue, royal blue or did he put all the blues together? What happened to the aquamarine? Did your artist have more—or less—trouble than your other subjects? Did anyone find it impossible to group the colors at all, insisting that each one was different from the others and in a class by itself? Did anyone make a single classification of all the blues and greens together in one pile? A Navajo might do this, because the Navajo language has no word for blue or for green, but only a single word that translates to blue-or-green.

The classes into which you choose to group objects often depend on the language you speak and, of course, your knowledge of it. What *one* word would you choose to describe all of the following:

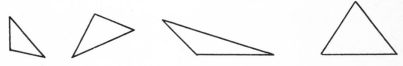

Did you say triangle? or figure? Do you have to notice more about the shapes to say "triangle" than to say "figure"?

What about this group:

Did you say "figure" or "simple closed curve"? You could not have said "simple closed curve" unless you know the term and have observed the figures closely enough to be sure that they all belong to that category. Do you perhaps rebel at the idea that a square is a curve? The mathematician and the sculptor may argue with each other about the meaning of words in their native language.

Does it seem ridiculous to you that the Hopi Indian language has only one word to cover everything that flies, except a bird, so that the same word may mean either an airplane, or an insect, or an aviator? The Eskimo might find it equally fantastic that English has only one word, "snow," to cover falling snow, snow on the ground, hard-packed snow, soupy snow, wind-driven swirls of snow. He might find it especially remarkable since English *has* separate words for rain, drizzle, fog, sleet, and hail.

For English-speaking people, the phrase "sister-in-law" means either a brother's wife or a husband's sister. An aunt may be a mother's sister, a father's sister, a mother's brother's wife, a father's brother's wife, or even an old friend of the family who is not closely related, if related at all. In countries where kinship is of greater importance than it is in our culture, this would be found to be hopelessly confusing, far worse than the aviator-airplane-insect grouping because you couldn't even figure out from context which relative was being described.

Before he can say, "I gave it to him" or "I dropped it," the Navajo child has to think of what kind of object was given or dropped. The verb he has to use will be different if the object is one of the long-object class (a pencil or a stick or a pipe), or in the things-bundled-up class (a bale of hay or a laundry bag), or a living thing, or a container-and-its-contents (sugar or salt), or one of a dozen other classifications. There are more than twenty words for "give" in Navajo, depending upon what it is you are giving. Now if you had to think in

English and translate into Navajo, this forced choice of the proper verb would slow you down. It doesn't slow the Navajo child down because it wouldn't occur to him to think in any other way. You, for instance, don't have any problem deciding whether to say "I stubbed my toe" or "I cut my toe" or "I skinned my toe" but someone whose language contained only the word "hurt" would be slowed down in translating.

Admittedly these are very minor examples of how the language we speak influences our thinking by selecting the categories into which we place what we see and hear about. But it is very difficult to give important examples to someone who speaks only one language (or a group of similar languages). If the theory that your thinking is limited by the kinds of words you have at hand to think with is correct, then what words can be used to prove to you that there are other ways of thinking? How well can you explain to a blind man the differences there are in various shades of color?

Consider how you think about time. In the United States and in the European countries from which many of our ancestors came, time is thought of as a continuing strip of something, beginning in the past, continuing in the present, and stretching on into the future like a tape. Perhaps in school you have drawn a time line and placed events in their proper spot upon it. Time, in the framework of English, is something that can be measured in minutes and hours in much the same way that distance can be measured in feet and inches. Sometimes we even use time as a measure of distance, saying that a town in Connecticut is "two hours from New York City." Arithmetic books are full of problems in which we add, subtract, multiply, and divide units of time. Time is something you have a measurable quantity of, like water in a tank. You can use it or save it. If you don't use the water in a tank, it's still there for later use. But suppose time is more like the water in a river. The amount of water that the river will carry past your house tomorrow is in no way affected by whether you draw out a bucketful today or you don't. Would this change your ideas about "saving" or "wasting" time?

Growing up speaking the English language with its built-in ideas of time requires you to set up all sorts of foolish equations. A years of a cat's life, we say, is more or less equal to seven years of a human's life. Is it? Perhaps it is in the sense that the average cat lives 10 or 11 years and the average human lives 70 or 80 years. But beyond that simple equivalence where does the statement lead? A one-year-old cat can be a mother but a seven-year-old girl certainly can't. Many cats live to the age of 15 or 16. Are they "really" 105 to 120 years old? Time is just not measured in the same way for the lives of all creatures. This is something our language ignores. It goes even farther by speaking in exactly the same words of living creatures and of things: a five-year-old child and a five-year-old car.

We bog down badly in our understanding of our language of time when we talk about events in different places. Did something that happened at 9 A.M. on January 7 in San Francisco happen at the same time as an event that took place at 9 A.M. on January 7 in New York? The educated answer is "No, there's a time zone difference." Fine, when you stop to analyze it, but when you listen to the news broadcast of what happened at a given time in the world, do you always translate it in terms of time zones? What exactly do you mean when you say that a "day" is shorter on Mars than on the earth?

The Hopi language has no words at all for time, in the sense that we speak of time. There is no exact way of saying five hours, ten days, two years. The Hopi Indian would explain to you that there is no way of experiencing ten days at one glance as you can experience ten feet. You cannot say, in Hopi, that you have a two-week vacation; you can say that you will go away and return on the fifteenth day. You cannot parcel out your life in years of past, present, and future. *What there was, what there is, exists and becomes later.* Different things, different creatures, become later in different ways. Some do so by growing, like plants. Some change, like caterpillars. Some endure in one shape until a violent force alters them, like trees until they are chopped down or burned. Some vanish swiftly, like smoke. Some disappear gradually, like rocks worn down by water. Time is different for all of these.

Time, in the Hopi language, varies with each observer, and there are no words that will allow the idea of two events occurring at the same time in different places. We speak of events occurring at "distant" places and also at "distant" times. In either case, the Hopi would say, it's "distant"—and therefore not "now," for "now" is "here and now."

Verbs in the Hopi language do not change as ours do to show present past and future. They change to show whether an event (past *or* present) is reported, whether what generally occurs—"dogs bark," for instance—is under discussion, or whether the speaker is telling of his hopes, intentions, or expectations of what will happen.

Instead of time as a measuring tape, there is time as a group of happenings that are prepared for, take place, are remembered, are desired, and prepared for. Everything that has ever happened, to the Hopi, still *is*. What is going to happen has already begun. Our clocks and calendars and record-keeping are of no use to him.

You can get some slight idea of this by asking yourself what you mean by "I" in the sentence "I used to eat Pablum." Are you the one who ate pablum? You, five feet four inches tall and weighing 110 pounds? Is there more logic in a language like the Sudanese African language, Mende, in which not the verb but the pronoun changes to show past, present, and future?

Another African language, Chichewa, has two past tenses—one for past events that influence the present and another for past events that have no present influence. Before you can say "I have eaten," you have to decide whether what you mean is, "I have eaten and so I'm not hungry and don't want to eat now" or "I have eaten but I'm still hungry." Within this framework there is a difference between past events that can be discovered by evidence that still exists (Here are the charred remains of a fire.) and those that exist only in memory (There was a white house with green shutters here before it burned down.). Consider the difference, in this language, in reporting to your teacher about yesterday's absence: "I was sick." Will your teacher say, "I'm glad you're better" or "Do you feel well enough to take the math test?" What kind of difference would thinking in this language make to philosophers, archaeologists, and scientists in general?

The language in which you do your thinking leads you to notice certain things and not others about the world around you. It tells you what to look for in order to name and classify. It controls what you report about what you observe. Of course you can learn to translate from one language to another, but that is not the point. While it is true that some ideas can be expressed more easily in one language than in another, that literal (word-for-word) translations from one language to another are often silly and meaningless, that is not the important difference. What is important is that the language you speak and think in makes it more likely that you will see things in a particular way, that you will *notice* whether the thread is blue or green, whether the snow is crusty or soft, whether what is past is of present importance.

Even in our own language the name we choose for an object or an idea affects our behavior toward it. Is it more dangerous to light a match when working near flammable liquids or inflammable liquids? In dividing 505 by 5 is the answer 11 because, since zero is "nothing," there's no need to put it down? Does the term "empty" lead you to believe that it would be safe to throw an "empty" butane gas tank on the fire?

Sometimes the language we use may make it difficult for us to see things in new ways. Not impossible, but difficult. We know that the earth revolves around the sun and that the sun does not "rise" or "set," but words like "sunrise" and "sunset" certainly don't make it easier to learn the facts. In describing a man to identify him, we speak of his height, weight, color of eyes, hair, facial features, scars, as if these were all similar qualities. A man with a thick head of hair in his youth may later be bald. Does an astronaut become weightless in outer space in the same way as he may become bald? Is weight a feature of the astronaut or is it a relationship between his mass and the mass of some other object such as the earth or the moon?

The structure of the English language requires every verb to have a subject even if the subject doesn't mean anything. We say "It is raining." What, exactly, is "it"? In this form it's unimportant, but this way of thinking has placed obstacles in the path of understanding science. We cannot say "flashed," as the Hopi can, without saying "a light flashed." But does this mean any more than "it" is raining? Is the "light" that flashed the same substance as the "light" that glowed or the "light" that was turned off? Is it a substance at all? The early chemists believed that anything that could burn must contain some fire stuff; they called it phlogiston. When a substance burned, phlogiston left it in the form of flame. The ash was the substance with the phlogiston removed.

It's the same kind of language problem that leads us to ask questions like "What makes it fall?" If you think of "gravity" as something that "makes" an object fall, you are going to have trouble with this situation: When a parachutist first jumps he moves with increasing speed but finally, still falling, he reaches a speed that does not change. At this point the force of air resistance and the force of gravity are both at work upon him. Which force is greater? If you believe that gravity is what "makes" him fall, you'll conclude that the force of gravity is greater. You'll be wrong. The forces are the same. Then, "What makes him fall?" Ask yourself a different question: What would make him stop falling?

If you think of a force as something that pushes or pulls and that pushing and pulling are *active* verbs then somebody or something must *do* something to exert a force. Then what do you do with this situation:

Tom and Harry are having a tug of war, pulling with all their force on the ends of a rope. They are equally matched. Harry has some chores to do but Tom wants to continue his tug-of-war activity. So Harry ties his end of the rope to a tree. Tom pulls his end with all his force. Is the rope now under the same tension as before? or less? Does the tree "pull" against Tom?

If this chapter seems more difficult than most it is because it *is* difficult to discuss color with a blind man. Language does limit and control our thinking and set the pattern for our understanding of the world around us. What do you mean, the Hopi Indian might ask you, when you say "the wind blows"? What is a wind when it doesn't blow?

VI

Unspeakable Ideas

☐

Babies babble endlessly. To the baby, "ga-ga," "ba-ba," "ca-ca" are all equally without meaning. But somewhere in this long string of meaningless syllables he happens to say "ma-ma." If his mother chances to be there to hear him, she becomes very excited because the baby has said his first word. She is especially pleased because his first word was her name. Certainly the baby recognizes her pleasure. He still does not know that he has said a word, much less what the word means, but he begins to know that out of that stream of sounds one particular sound is special and that he will be rewarded by his mother's pleasure if he makes the sound again.

When he continues in his repetitive chant of "day-day," "pay-pay," "may-may," "lay-lay" nothing happens in the life of the child of English-speaking parents to cause him to choose one of these sounds over another. But the baby of French-speaking parents will find his mother overjoyed to realize that the baby has now learned another word and—amazing—is asking for milk. *"Lait"* (pronounced "lay") is the French word for milk. The French baby, being given milk when he says "lay-lay," will soon learn that this is a useful sound to make. "Lay-lay" produced nothing for the child of English-speaking parents, so he has no reason to prefer it over "may-may" or "bay-bay." "Bay-bay," indeed, may be the preferred one, for someone may decide he is trying to say "baby." The French parents will chalk up another word to the infant's credit: *"bébé"* (pronounced "bay-bay") is French for baby. As the baby grows, he begins to get the idea that words and things or people are somehow related, that saying the name of the thing or person often produces what is named. Pretty soon he will point to things and ask to be told their names.

Learning to speak a language properly is really a very difficult undertaking, as you discover when you try to learn a second language—and learning a second language is a much easier job than learning the idea of language in the first place. To learn, for example, that if someone says "you," he means the person you have been referring to as "me," but that if *you* say "you," you're talking about someone other than yourself, is really a very complicated bit of reasoning for a two-year-old. But he manages it. He makes mistakes, of course. He says charming phrases like "both of me" for "both of us." Not yet plunged into the crazy pattern of irregular verbs he says, quite logically, "I breaked it" or "I sleeped." But he learns, accepting fully the pattern of speech he hears. And, along with names for table and man and horse, he learns the meaning of words like justice and courage and happiness. With these he learns what his parents, his teachers and his social community consider to be the important things to know, to speak of, to think about.

There are bound to be words to go with the things and

ideas that are to be spoken about or thought about. The most important things and ideas, the ones most frequently needed and used, have simple words to express them. As in a well-ordered workshop where the tools most often used are kept handy, and are usually the simplest, the most needed words are short and simple: "I," "you," "he," "is," "go," "come," "do," "for," "by," and so on. If a thing has a long and complicated name to begin with, the name is usually shortened if the thing becomes one that is used and talked about daily. The "automobile" becomes the "car," the "television set" becomes "TV" (or the "telly" in England), the "refrigerator" becomes the "frig," the "gymnasium" is the "gym," the "veterinarian" is the "vet."

By looking at the length of the names of objects or ideas in a language, it is possible to make a fair guess about the life in the community that uses the language and about what is considered important to the people. Sometimes it is a general term that is most frequently used: you are more likely to run home yelling, "A dog bit me" than "A cocker spaniel bit me." But this is not always the case. You are more likely to say, "It's raining" or "It's hailing" or "It's snowing" than to say, "There's precipitation in the air." "Rain" and "snow," like "dog," are the simplest tools at hand.

While it is not impossible for you to speak of things and ideas whose names are complicated to express, you're less likely to do so. Of course, if it's important to the story, you can say, "A cocker spaniel bit me," but normally you wouldn't. If, however, your language contained no word for "dog" in general, but only the names of each of the breeds, you'd have to tell about the cocker spaniel. English, for example, requires you to distinguish between brother and sister, for there is no ordinary word which means "either brother or sister." (There is a formal word for this—sibling—but you'd sound rather odd if you said to your teacher, "I don't have to take that notice home to my parents because my sibling got one yesterday.") By contrast, there's no convenient way in English of saying whether the cousin you're talking about is a boy or a girl.

As you have seen in the last chapter, languages differ greatly in the demands they make upon you, and in what you must notice in order to report your experience in words. An overseer, making the rounds of a ranch, can report in English that one of the fences is broken. Speaking in Navajo, he would have to decide first whether the fence had been broken by a human on the one hand or by an animal or a natural force on the other, because there is no single word "broken" that would apply to both.

The language spoken by any group of people contains all the words that the group feels are needed. The existence of a word in a language is no guarantee that the thing it names exists; we have words, for example, for flying saucers and unicorns, ghosts, witches, and fairies. But if the language does not contain a word to name an object it is fair to assume either that the people do not know of the object or that they consider the object not worth mentioning or thinking about. If there is no word in the language for automobile, there are probably no automobiles in the community. If there is no word for uncle, it doesn't follow that there are no uncles, but you can conclude that the relationship of uncle is not considered important. In English, for instance, there is no convenient way to refer to the mother-in-law of one's sister, but other languages do have a word for this.

New words or phrases are added to a language when

the need for them is felt. Of course new inventions have to have names, but there are other things and ideas that are not new, just newly important—for example, "girl friend" and "boy friend." "Friend" alone did well enough for English-speaking people for hundreds of years. It isn't sufficient nowadays. Stop and think what changes have occurred in our manners and customs in the last few hundred years to bring about this need for a change in language. And the likelihood is that a new word will soon come into being, for "girl friend" now has two quite different meanings, depending upon whether it is used by a girl or by a boy to refer to a friend.

In these days when it is quite common for young men and women, at college or at their first jobs, to live away from their parents' homes in houses or apartments that they rent together, some word other than "roommate" is clearly needed. And perhaps the language will begin to recognize what one man described as a "house husband" (to match housewife), to describe the man who takes care of the house and the children because he is studying or working at home while his wife has a job outside of the home. In time, if these relationships remain important to the community, some simple terms will be invented to name them.

Some words are missing from the language because discussion of some subjects is considered improper or impolite. Only medical terms, baby talk, and "dirty words" exist to describe certain bodily functions. If there are no ordinary, everyday words for things, a person is less likely to talk about or even to think about them. A study of the things not named in a language, or of the names not allowed to be spoken, can give a very accurate picture of the customs and morals of the community.

When there are no available or acceptable names to

be used, it often happens that euphemisms arise to take their place. A euphemism is a polite substitute for a word that is supposed to be avoided. As mentioned earlier, you don't ever kill your incurably sick pet; you "put it to sleep." Those killed in war are "casualties." There are many euphemisms for death.

In time of war, people avoid reference to the enemy and avoid the use of the enemy's language in ordinary conversation in any form that is not hostile. During World War I, sauerkraut was referred to as "liberty cabbage," and even German measles was out, being renamed "liberty measles," though the logic of this euphemism is pretty hard to justify.

Try to find a "small" box of detergent or a "small" tube of toothpaste. Unless what is being presented is a "pocket size" so that convenience in carrying is emphasized, the small size will probably be labeled "personal" or "regular" or perhaps even "large." If you really want the large size, look for the "giant" or "jumbo" or "family" size. On television there are no advertisements. There are only "messages," "announcements," and, of course "pauses for station identification," which include a minimum of three "commercials." Employees and officials of companies are seldom fired. Instead, they are requested to resign. In general, the unpleasant is avoided.

Where the unpleasant is also considered impolite, the euphemisms are even more numerous. The *Dictionary of American Slang* lists over 200 words for toilet! But even without resorting to slang, think how many euphemisms there are : washroom, bathroom, ladies' or men's room, powder room, lounge, restroom, lavatory, to name just the most obvious. Notice that these either do not mention at all what the room is for (ladies' room) or lead you to believe that it's just a place to wash or relax. Even the word toilet itself—now the basic word and not considered very polite—comes from the French *"toilette,"* which has to do with dressing and grooming. The French meaning survives in English in the phrase "toilet water," a slightly perfumed liquid used in or after a bath. *"Toilette"* in French doesn't mean "toilet" in our sense at all. They have different words for the "convenience."

Sometimes a subject is so far out-of-bounds that words that even *suggest* the subject are shunned. In Victorian times, it was considered improper to refer to leg of lamb or to ask for breast of chicken. Only a few years ago a group of six men, American musicians, were incorrectly referred to as a quintet because the correct term, sextet, might prove embarrassing. Have you known people who blushed when talking about dams?

In some primitive communities, such as some of those of the African Bantu tribes, where there is a taboo, a prohibition, that forbids a woman to mention her husband's name, she must also avoid pronouncing any words that sound like his name. If this were the rule in our language, a woman whose husband's name was Robert could not speak of robbers or say that a cork bobbed on the water or ask for a bobbin for her sewing machine.

Forbidden language is usually associated with taboos of this kind. The word "taboo" itself comes from the Polynesian languages of the Pacific Islands where there are very many actions and words that are forbidden by the native religion and culture. Most primitive people are required to respect numerous taboos. There are forbidden foods, prohibited relationships between persons of the same tribe, words that may not be spoken or hinted at, things that may not be handled at all or may be used only in certain approved ways.

But taboos are certainly not limited to primitive communities. We have quite a few of our own, some in our religions, some in social customs. In India you cannot eat the meat of a cow; in America you cannot eat the meat of a horse. A man must remove his hat in a church, but he may not in a synagogue.

Swearing is among the taboos of our culture, and that is why many euphemisms for swear words are common. Most of them have no meaning in themselves and are used because they sound like swear words or, at least, start with the same letters. "Aw, heck" and "darn it" are familiar examples. About thirty years ago, the practice of censorship of "bad" words in books was flourishing. When the writer wanted to tell the reader that the character in his novel was using "bad" language he was not permitted to print the words his character uttered. Instead, the whole word (or all of it except the first letter) would be printed in asterisks or dashes. The result, as you might expect, was the opposite of what the high-minded censors intended. Just as the sign "for adults only" draws crowds of teen-agers to the doors of a movie house, so the asterisks set people to wondering what were the awful words that were omitted. Probably some of the ideas that came to mind were far worse than what the author intended. Consider, for example, what censorship of that kind would do a first-grade reader:

> Look, Jane, look!
> See Dick *******
> Run, Jane, run!

These days there are fewer restrictions on the use of language, fewer unspeakable thoughts. Does the fact that language is freer produce freer behavior? Or is the language freer because the behavior is more open? Let's say the two go hand in hand.

Not only the laws of a community, not only its social customs, but also, and especially, its language tell you how to behave, how to think about the world and how to describe it. You need words to think with and if you don't have the words for an object or an action or a relationship, you are less likely—if not completely unable —to think about it. This chapter is largely about unspeakable ideas of other times or other places, for what words could be used to discuss the unspeakable ideas of here and now?

VII

The Clash of Symbols

☐

What is the meaning of a red flag at the end of a ladder sticking out at the back of a pick-up truck? Does it mean that the driver is a Communist? Words have different meanings in different contexts—you don't put your money in a river bank. So do symbols. In the theater, a red light means "This way out." On the highway, it means "Stop!" Is there anything special about the color red for any of these uses? Could a green light stand for "Stop!"?

What does the sound of a siren symbolize? Where you live, a siren might mean an ambulance or a fire engine. To a friend from another country, it might mean an air raid alarm. Suppose the two of you are off on a trip to another country. You are walking down the street of a town unfamiliar to both of you. You hear a siren. Do you both react in the same way?

Or suppose your friend has grown up in Vietnam, where the sight or sound of a low-flying plane signals a bombing raid. How long will it take him, living now in your town, to learn that low-flying planes are just coming in for a landing at the nearby airport, that he needn't dive under the table, that not all low-flying planes mean death?

You have been trained from a very early age to respond to symbols in appropriate ways. Many of these responses must be automatic, unthinking, because speed in responding may be a matter of life and death. Some symbols— like the skull and crossbones of the poison label—must be taken on faith, because it's not a good idea to try tasting the substance to find out if it's really poisonous. Others, like merit badges, can be questioned: Does that Girl Scout really know how to cook well?

Some symbols are signs and nothing more. They have no use in themselves except to represent an idea, a command, a direction. The flag, the siren, the poison label, and the badge are of this kind. There's a cross on the top of the structure? It's a church. There's a six-pointed star? It's a synagogue. There's an S? The road will curve.

The most familiar symbol of this type is money. Once upon a time, as they say in children's books, there was no such thing as money. If you had more sheep than you needed, you might trade a sheep for a pig. If you kept the extra sheep, you might trade the wool for some potatoes. Barter—the exchange of goods for other goods— was the normal way of doing business. Money was invented very early in man's history. It was just too much trouble to lead the extra sheep around from town to town in search of someone who was similarly leading a pig around to swap for a sheep. Some pieces of metal, or shell, or whatever, could be used to symbolize the value of the sheep and the pig. In this way, three-way, five-way, 1000-way exchanges were made possible. What was important here was to ensure that everybody who was involved in any of the exchanges would recognize that the pieces of metal or shell were indeed worth the value of the sheep, the pig, the wool, and the potatoes.

There are two ways of ensuring this. One is for the money—whatever form it takes—to have intrinsic value, that is to say that the amount of copper or silver or gold in the coin is generally acknowledged to be worth as much as the face value of the coin. A ten-dollar gold piece would thus have to contain ten dollars' worth of gold. But if it did, what way would be found to pay for the work of turning the gold into a coin? Could you possibly persuade a metal worker to make you something as intricate as a copper penny for the price of one cent, materials included? By and large, this method of ensuring the value of money won't work. The second method is for everyone to agree that someone they trust is keeping track of the exchanges.

Sometimes this is the government. It can issue money printed on paper, which has very little value in itself. The paper is a symbol, once for the gold the government was presumed to be keeping in hidden vaults, now for the ability of the government to collect that much value of goods and services if it's called on to do so. Sometimes a bank is the one chosen to keep track of the exchanges. Just one piece of paper (and not even very good paper), when written as a check, can symbolize thousands of pieces of paper money, or the reserve of gold or silver behind it, or the work of the potato growers back of that. The check is the symbol of the symbol (paper money) of the symbol (precious metal) of the work of planting and digging the potatoes.

But this system has to function on trust. Why will a storekeeper cash your check only if he knows you or is satisfied with your identification? Why do you sometimes have trouble using a Canadian dime in the United States? Would you be able to buy anything in your local supermarket with French francs or Italian lira or German marks?

Behind every symbol there has to be agreement about what it symbolizes. Otherwise the symbol fails as a symbol. What will you do when, driving along the highway, you see a blue traffic light?

Some symbols are not *just* symbols. They have other uses besides, and then it is not always easy to be sure which use is the more important. Clothing is an easy example. Some clothing is intended to be mainly symbolic. Why do policemen wear uniforms? If you need a policeman, how practical would it be for you to approach each man you see in the street and ask if he's a policeman? Why do certain policemen—plainclothesmen—*not* wear uniforms? Would it be convenient if all doctors were required to wear red overalls? Why might a doctor object to doing so?

Uniforms are easy to recognize and highly useful. The woman alone in the house will not open her door to a strange man, unless, of course, he's wearing the uniform of the electric company's meter reader. A strange woman hands you a cup of some bad-smelling stuff and says, "Drink it!" You will if she's wearing the uniform of a nurse.

But it's not only uniforms that symbolize a person's occupation, profession, or status. Other clothing does too. In other times and places there were standards that had to be obeyed. Purple was a royal color and ermine a royal fur, and no commoner could wear either. In early New England, a woman was allowed to wear a silk scarf only if her husband was "worth" $1,000. These days there are no such rules. Anyone may wear a mink coat, but who are the people who can? Anyone can buy and wear a black leather jacket, but who are the people who do? Why is a kitchen apron a suitable protection for a girl who is helping her mother wash the dishes, but not for her brother? A diaper would serve exactly the same purpose as the lower half of a bikini. Why don't you see diapers on girls at the beaches?

Clothing, cars, house furnishings, the houses they furnish, all are useful in themselves but all are also symbols of the status of their owners. Does the lady wear a mink coat because it's warm? Yes, partly. But is it a thousand times warmer than a coat made of reprocessed wool? Is a new Cadillac that much better a means of transportation than a three-year-old Chevy? What of the song writer who spent nearly half a million dollars furnishing his $275,000 penthouse on New York's Fifth Avenue?

Jewelry isn't as plainly useful as clothing, but it does satisfy the desire for beauty. So do paintings and tapestries and sculpture. But why is it so important whether the diamonds are real? Of course, if jewelry looks shoddy, it's not beautiful, but suppose it takes a diamond expert to tell whether it's real or fake? If you have to ask whether the painting is an original or a reproduction, why does it matter which it is? From what point of view is the first edition of a book of more value than the second?

Status symbols play an extremely large part in our society. They are the basis of much of the advertising we read and listen to. This is what rich people wear; wouldn't you like to look rich? This is where rich people go; wouldn't you like to be thought to be a member of the jet set?

Association of the symbol with a particular status may create confusion between cause and effect. Chanticleer, the rooster in the old fable, always began crowing just before dawn. He crowed and then the sun rose. Poor befuddled rooster! He thought it was he who made the sun rise. When it rains hard, you see the streets crowded with people wearing raincoats and carrying umbrellas. Do you conclude that donning a raincoat and opening an umbrella makes it rain? Rich and important people drive around in Cadillacs. Will driving a Cadillac make you rich and important? It might make you feel that way. It might make other people think of you that way.

"You get a feeling of assurance behind an Itkin desk," says a newspaper ad, "This desk speaks so highly of you. 'He's sound,' it says. 'A man of taste . . . good judgment'."

"If you want to know the kind of man he is," reads another ad, "take a look at the car he drives. This car is in a class by itself. But then again, so is the man who drives it."

Expensive cars, a costly house at a "good address," luxurious furnishings—these are status symbols intended to convey to people a man meets in business or socially that he has made it, that he's up there with the kings and the king makers. The *symbol* of the status is often all that is required. If you have the symbol firmly in hand, you don't really need what it symbolizes.

Is it important to be a successful athlete or is it the letter to sew on your sweater that you really want? If you could buy the letter, would you? There are stores whose business is selling trophies. They'll engrave any name and date you order. Would you buy yourself a bowling championship? Do you know people who cheat on exams in order to make the honor roll? Do you know people who change the grades on their tests and report cards? Clothing from expensive stores may be more carefully tailored of better material than merchandise in lower-priced stores. If there's a sale of coats from such a store, with the labels cut out, will you buy a coat? If you could buy just the label, would you? These last two questions can be answered in a variety of ways. Can you justify your answers to yourself? to someone else? One of the plushiest gift shops in New York is selling empty gift boxes with the firm name printed on it. $10 a box. Would you buy one?

Do you want to be an adult? to seem to be an adult? to be treated as an adult? What are the symbols of adult status? Which of these could you acquire before you are an adult? Are the symbols alone worth having? and if so, why?

What do you make of this story of a small community, Briar Park, in the town on Wantagh, Long Island, a "good address"? A developer bought up a large tract of land that completely surrounded the community. His development was big enough to rate its own village name, Levittown, and its own post office. There could be lots of reasons why the original community of Briar Park refused to adopt the new town name as their address. But why wouldn't they accept mail delivered by the Levittown post office? Evidently, postal officials said, a Wantagh address requires a Wantagh postman. And so, by demand of Briar Park, Wantagh postmen walk through Levittown to deliver Briar Park mail.

All kinds of odd results occur when the symbol is confused with the thing it symbolizes, or when you simply don't stop to ask whether it is the workmanship of the coat or the label that you really want.

Among German University students in the nineteenth and early twentieth century, dueling, long outlawed in other civilized countries, persisted as a status sport. A dueling scar across the cheek was a mark of honor. How about a scar cut to order in the most becoming spot? Is there such a thing as a "strong chin"? Would it do to wear a false one? Is hair on the chest a symbol of virility in men? Would false hair on the chest really be ridiculous? different from false eyelashes? What's your view of white-wall tires? of paste-on rims to simulate white-wall tires?

What is the value of a false symbol—counterfeit money, a check that bounces? It rather depends on what you do with it, doesn't it? Put a veneer of stone on the front of your house to replace the shoddy asbestos siding. No harm done if someone's fooled into thinking it's a stone house. Paste diamonds? Fake fireplaces? What does it matter? How about stone veneer on a wooden bridge?

How real in your mind does a symbol become and how does its fake reality affect your dealing with it? A child loves a stuffed toy because it's soft and cuddly and comforting. So is a pillow, but there's a difference. If the pillow becomes dirty and lumpy and begins to lose its stuffing, you can tell the child to take it down and throw it in the garbage pail. He will, without a qualm. But don't tell him to do the same with his dirty, lumpy, worn-out teddy bear that's losing its stuffing. The symbol has *become* the thing it symbolizes.

Among primitive people, even today, the confusion

of the symbol with what it symbolizes is common, and dangerous. Make a rag doll to be an effigy of your enemy and you have him in your power. You can kill him by sticking pins into the heart of your rag doll effigy. In a New York City store today you can buy yourself a voodoo kit—a rag doll and a set of gold-plated sewing needles to hex your enemy. The same store will sell you powder to rub on your body to cure whatever problems you have, green candles to bring money, black candles to drive away your enemies, red candles to attract a boy friend, and purple candles to control the thoughts and actions of anyone you choose. But choose wisely. Choose someone as your victim who believes that the magic works. If your victim is convinced that you can kill him by sticking pins into a rag doll, or by the black and purple candles you burn, there's a very good chance that, if he doesn't die, he'll at least become very sick. Can one be "worried to death"? truly *worried* to death? Yes, it is possible.

One can be as easily cured as killed. When a new medicine is being tested to see if it will be an effective cure for certain diseases, medical researchers will often ask doctors to give the medicine in capsule form to some of their patients and to give placebos to others. A placebo is a capsule that looks just like the real medicine capsule but in fact contains nothing of any curative value whatever. If the doctor himself cannot tell them apart and if he gives the placebo to a patient, telling him what a wonderful new miracle cure it is, the patient may be cured just as effectively as if he had been given the real medicine. Naturally, it depends on what the disease is, but, above all, the patient has to believe that he has swallowed the real medicine. He is more likely to believe this if the doctor believes it too.

Of course, this isn't the usual occurrence. Mostly, people do know the difference between the symbol and the real thing. Very few of us will be content to sleep under the picture of a blanket, nor will we reach into the artistic bowl of artificial fruit when we're hungry. The placebo and the voodoo doll are extreme examples of confusing the symbol with the thing symbolized. But there are other examples, less dramatic perhaps, but equally astonishing.

Most people know that inherited characteristics are a matter of genes, that "bad blood" is an unscientific metaphor, like "sunrise." Nobody would expect royalty to bleed "blue blood" nor does anyone take the term "Negro blood" literally. Are you sure? During World War II, although there was a great need of blood donors for plasma for the battlefields, the Red Cross was forced by a substantial public demand to set up separate blood banks for "white" and "Negro" blood lest the blood of some white soldier be "contaminated" with "Negro blood."

Suppose your friend Bill is describing an imaginary battle. "Look," he says to you, "this sugar bowl is the Empire State Building and these forks are jets." The battle scene goes along at a great pace until suddenly a fork drops and chips the sugar bowl. If a wail goes up from Bill's mother because an expensive sugar bowl's been damaged, that makes sense. If she starts to phone the police to tell them that a jet has crashed into the Empire State Building, it won't make sense even to Bill, despite the fact that he's been saying all along that the sugar bowl *is* the Empire State Building. He doesn't expect to be taken that seriously. He didn't mean it that way, naturally.

But often symbols do get out of hand and people do take them seriously in just that way. For instance, take the human heart. Its actual job is to pump blood through the body, and if it stops beating for too long, you die. Also, the speed and regularity of its beat is an indication of the state of your health, because it will beat more slowly or faster than normal, depending on how you're feeling, either physically or emotionally. So expressions like, "I was so excited that my heart stopped beating" may be slightly exaggerated but they are meant to be taken seriously and are not symbolic. But how about the phrase, "My heart belongs to Daddy," or "I'm broken-hearted," "I'll die of a broken heart," "My heart's in the highlands; my heart is not here"? These phrases have nothing really to do with the heart at all, have they? They mean "I love Daddy best," "I am disappointed in love," "I love the highlands and would rather be there than here where I am." In all these phrases, the heart is used as a symbol for "love" of various kinds and it has nothing whatever to do with the blood pump. The doctor is no more going to respond to a call to sew up a broken heart than the police are to come dashing out with a rescue squad when the sugar-bowl-Empire-State-Building is hit by a fork-jet-plane. Maybe you think this is so obvious that it's not worth mentioning. Six-year-old stuff. Agreed. But then consider this article from *The New York Times* of June 15, 1953:

JAN PADEREWSKI'S HEART
TO STAY IN THIS COUNTRY

The heart of Jan Paderewski, pianist-composer-statesman, will remain in the United States, despite superficial changes in Soviet foreign policy, it was announced yesterday. The Polish pianist's will specified that his heart was to remain in this country until Communist control of his homeland had ended.

The executor of the will died last month and the new executor, Edward F. G. Imperatore, a Brooklyn lawyer, said yesterday that the heart would remain in its Cypress Hills crypt until Poland "has resumed its rightful place among the free and independent nations of the world." The rest of M. Paderewski's body is buried in Arlington National Cemetery.

Well? Does it make sense? And yet, in other matters, M. Paderewski definitely did make sense. He got carried away by a symbol. So have all of us, sometime or other.

What about flags? Are they pieces of cloth that you can buy for almost any price you care to spend, or are they the country they symbolize? If a flag falls down in the street and somebody tramples on it, is it a piece of cloth that got dirty, perhaps hopelessly, so that it's ruined and you'll have to spend money to replace it (like the sugar bowl), or is it a vital blow to the country it stands for? Does it matter whether the trampling was deliberate or accidental? Would you risk your life to save a flag? If so, why would you?

Why is it more of a crime to burn a draft card than to burn any other identification, or a piece of cardboard the same size and shape?

Parents don't punish their children as often or as severely as they once did. But not so long ago the punishment for saying "dirty words," for "having a dirty mouth" was to wash that dirty mouth with soap. And if, by any chance, that remedy really works, please go promptly to the nearest supermarket, buy a good whisk broom and brush the cobwebs from your mind. For your mind is full of words, and words are the commonest symbols of all, the most misleading, the most often confused with the things they symbolize.

VIII

How to Translate English

☐

It is perfectly possible to answer questions correctly without knowing what either the question or the answer means. People who have this skill—and it is easy to acquire—often do spectacularly well on standardized school tests. Some of them grow up to become writers of political campaign speeches or ads for indigestion remedies.

Let's see what aptitude you have in this area. Try yourself on the following text. Read it and answer the multiple choice questions:

Because public opinion is sometimes marsiflate, empetricious insoculences are frequently zophili-mized. Nevertheless, it cannot be overemphasized that carpoflansibles are highly traculate.

1. In the author's opinion, carpoflansibles are
   (a) empetricious
   (b) traculate
   (c) zophilimized

2. Public opinion is sometimes
   - (a) insoculent
   - (b) variable
   - (c) marsiflate
3. According to the text, insoculences are zophili-mized
   - (a) often
   - (b) never
   - (c) sometimes

The correct answers, as you surely know, are 1b, 2c, 3a. But what is the paragraph all about? Is it desirable to zophilimize an empetricious insoculence? Don't reach for the dictionary, it will not enlighten you. Besides, why do you need to know? You've answered the questions correctly, haven't you? What more do you want?

The words, of course, are pure gibberish, invented for the purpose. But stop a minute. Do you really know any more about what "public opinion" is than about what an "insoculence" is? You can find "public opinion" in the dictionary: "The predominant attitude of a com-munity: the collective will of the people." Does that help? Are you one of the many people who believe that if they have defined a word they know what it means?

There is always the question of context. If you look in a Spanish-English dictionary you'll find the word "*querer*" defined as "to want, to desire, to love." Does that cause confusion? Will it be impossible to discover whether a man is saying "I want my secretary" or "I love my secretary"? Spanish-speaking people are not confused. They might be confused, though, by hearing an Ameri-can say on three different occasions: "I love my mother," "I love my wife," "I love chocolate ice cream." If someone asks you to define "batter" and "pitcher" and "plate," you'd better inquire whether he's thinking of the ball field or the kitchen, but once this has been established, no one is really likely to be confused. But in many cases it's not simply a question of choosing the right definition for the context. The words that are tricky are the ones that mean almost the same thing—but not quite—in different contexts.

Take the word "law." Define it as a group of rules that must be obeyed? Not bad. But what differences of meaning are there when the word is used in the following phrases?

We need more law and order in this town.
the law of averages
What does the new tax law require?
The Constitution is the law of the land.
law of nature
I'll have the law on you.
law of the jungle
law of gravity
lay down the law

A lawbreaker is a criminal who breaks the law. Which of these laws can he break? Can a law be repealed? Which of these laws can? Does the word law arouse feelings of awe, respect, and duty? Can that feeling confuse the issue?

As Americans, we're very fond of the words "free" and "freedom." We fight to "preserve the free world," to oppose dictatorship. But does the "free world" include the dictatorships of Latin America, of Spain and Portugal

and South Vietnam? What exactly is the "Free World"?
"Free" in what sense?

What do we mean by "free" anyway? Is it perhaps a
word like "law"? How are "free" and "freedom" used in
these well-accepted phrases:

free admission
free ride
free speech
free as a bird
free act
free and easy
freedom from fear
free of impurities
Are you free for lunch?
The best things in life are free.
Lincoln set the slaves free.
free verse

Basically, there are three meanings here. One is best
translated as "happily without." In this sense one is free
from something else—from fear, from imperfections,
from hunger. Second, we use the word to mean that
there's no money to be paid, as in "free admission," but
sometimes we mean that there's nothing at all to be
sacrificed, as in the slang use of "free ride." Third, when
you're free to be yourself, you mean that nothing's holding you back, you're "free as a bird"; it's your free act
when no one's making you do it. No restraints, no com-
pulsions, or, like "free verse," no rules (about rhyme and
meter) that have to be obeyed.

Three quite different ideas are thus packed up in one
word. The famous "four freedoms" of World War II—

freedom from hunger, freedom from fear, freedom of speech, and freedom of worship—led one to believe that the same kind of freedom was involved in all four, but was it?

Suppose we agree that the main kind of freedom we intend in the phrase "free world" is freedom from restraint or compulsion. What kind of restraint? If your hands and feet are tied and your mouth is gagged, it's clear you're not free. If you're in jail or a slave, you're not free. But suppose the restraints are not so clear cut. If someone has taken away all your clothes and then tells you that you are free to go anywhere you like, are you? Suppose that, instead of having all your clothes taken away, you simply have no money to buy clothes and no way of getting any? In what sense are you free to eat dinner at the best restaurants? to fly to Paris? to buy a yacht?

Are you free to do something if nobody will stop you from doing it but you know you will be punished later? Are you free to cut classes? Are you free to drive at 100 miles per hour along the highway? Are you free to speak if you are punished for what you say? How big does the punishment have to be before your freedom to do something is gone? Is a man always free to quit his job? Is a student always free to tell his teacher he thinks he's incompetent?

This sign really was displayed in a drugstore in Washington, D.C.

AMERICA——THE LAND OF FREEDOM
Where everyone is free to choose between
nationally advertised brands

How much of a choice is necessary for the choice to be free? Is an election free when there is only one candidate for whom one is free to vote "yes" or "no"? Is it free if there are two candidates to choose between? Suppose neither one supports the stand you'd like to vote for?

What about "freedom of the press"? Is freedom from censorship by the government enough? Does it matter how many newspapers there are? How many owners of newspapers? Does it matter what it costs to start a newspaper of general circulation in a fair-sized city?

You can play the definition game on your own. Try "democratic" and "democracy" for a starter. Bear in mind that in World War I we fought to "save the world for democracy" with the Czar as our ally.

It's not only words of high-sounding principle, not only slogans and rallying cries that cause confusion. Some of the smallest and most frequently used words are among those that cause the most trouble. "Is"—a word so obvious in meaning that no one bothers to define it—is one of the worst culprits. It's difficult to get along without it but, to see some of the different meanings it can have, try to rewrite each of these sentences without using it:

1. A horse is a four-legged animal.
2. 6 is the product of 3 × 2.
3. This painting is beautiful.
4. My father is a salesman.
5. My mother is the best mother in the world.

The first sentence could be rewritten: "We have agreed to represent a group of four-legged animals of a certain kind by the name 'horse'; the French call the same animal '*cheval*,' and the Germans call it '*Pferd*'; other four-legged animals have other names." For the second sentence we could say something like this: "We have agreed that if we select two objects at a time on three occasions, we will have selected a number of objects that we will call '6,' the symbol used all over the world with different sounds to express it."

In both cases, the "is" is definitional and, at first sight, both sentences seem to be of the same type—a matter of agreement about name. Not quite, though. Not all four-legged animals are horses. All products of 3×2 are 6. The definition of "6" is reversible; that of "horse" is not.

This "we have agreed" approach won't fit the third sentence. If people agree on the meaning of "2" and "3" and "x," then they must agree on the meaning of "3×2" and need only find a word to stand for "6." But people can agree on the meaning of "painting" and a word to stand for "beautiful" without agreeing that a particular painting "is" beautiful.

The sentence "My father is a salesman" looks like a definition, but it isn't. "My father is a man," "My father is forty-two years old," "My father is my mother's husband" may all be true, but none of these *defines* my father. Sentence number four can best be rewritten: "My father earns a living by selling things."

The fifth sentence is best rendered: "I love my mother." "Is" has no place in it.

In which of the five categories would you place each of the following? Or do you find other categories?

Honesty is the best policy.
This is a book about the uses of language.

$\sqrt{-1}$ is an imaginary number.

Murder is a crime.

A refrigerator is a box or room for keeping things cool.

The constitution is the law of the land.

A repeating decimal is a decimal fraction in which only a single figure recurs.

"Is" can cause as much confusion in questions as in statements. When someone asks "What is that?" the problem is only partly that of how to define "that." It is also a question of whether the "is" calls for a name, a function, a classification, a description, an opinion, or none of these. In order to know what the question calls for, you must first ask, "Who wants to know?" For instance, "What's water?" What answer should you give if the question is asked by

a Frenchman who doesn't speak English?

a 15-month-old child?

a chemistry teacher?

a man who has just asked you if there's anything to drink in the house and you've said, "Yes, water."

Sometimes the answer to the question "Who wants to know?" is: Nobody. Not all sentences ending with question marks are questions, despite what it says in the grammar books. Some are commands: "Will you please keep quiet?," "Will you answer the telephone?" Some are expressions of anger or reproach: "What on earth do you think you're doing?" "Who do you think you are?" Some are statements cast in the form of rhetorical questions: "What is so rare as a day in June?" "Will there ever be an end to crime?" (And some of these are wholly illogical, as when "Isn't it a beautiful day?" means that it *is* a beautiful day.) Some questions are nothing more than greetings: "How do you do?" "How are you?" Some are nagging, pleading statements: "Why can't I, Mommy, why?" The last thing the child wants at that point is to be told *why* he can't do whatever it is he wants to do.

If you know a five-year-old, you've probably had a conversation pretty much like this one:

Why are we getting off here?

Because this is the bus stop nearest Aunt Mary's house.

Why?

Because this is Thirty-second Street and Aunt Mary lives at Thirty-first Street and the bus stops only at every other block.

Why?

Because it takes time to stop and let people on and off, and when it stops it's not moving and so it isn't getting where it's going.

Why?

Oh, shut up!

"Oh, shut up!" is a perfectly suitable answer. Suppose you wanted to be nice and polite. What could you possibly say in answer to that last "Why?" that you hadn't already said? Was the child really asking for information when he asked the fifth "Why?" The fourth? The third?

A lot of time is wasted when people assume that because something looks or sounds like a question, it is one.

Some questions just can't be answered. To take some extreme examples:

> What is the thickness of anger?
> Who first discovered water?

These are obvious nonsense. But some almost equally nonsensical questions have been given serious consideration for long periods of time: What is truth? What is the meaning of meaning? "How many planets ought there to be?" was one that philosophers argued about not so many centuries ago. "Is a sound a sound if nobody hears it?" still finds its way into college bull sessions.

For a question to be meaningful, some thinkers say, there has to be the possibility of making some observations that could answer it. While this may be true of questions of fact, there are other questions that can never be answered by observation but only by faith— "Is there a heaven?"—or by exchange of opinion—"What is the best form of government for a town?"—or by definition of terms—"What is the square root of three?"

If you simply want to answer a question correctly, somebody will probably tell you what answer to give: Public opinion is sometimes marsiflate. But if you want to know what the question means, you will first have to find out who's asking it, what *he* means by the words he uses, whether he really wants an answer, whether it's a question about observable fact, a question of opinion or faith, or a question of definition where the asker is seeking to discover what the agreement is among some particular group of people about what the word shall be used to mean. In that way, you will be better able to understand the question, but you're not necessarily going to be closer to the "right" answer.

Translating English isn't an easy task. Don't words have meanings, then? Humpty Dumpty and Alice had an argument on the subject. Alice objected when Humpty Dumpty said he was using "glory" to mean "a nice knock-down argument."

"The question is," said Alice, "whether you *can* make a word mean so many different things."

"The question," said Humpty Dumpty, "is which is to be master—that's all."

It is possible to take Humpty Dumpty's side of the argument. Words are tools and, like tools, you can use them for whatever purpose may suit you. If you have a chisel, there's nothing to prevent your using it as a screwdriver. But if you do, you'll chip and blunt its edge and pretty soon it won't be a very good chisel. But, while it will be too blunt for a chisel, it will still be too sharp to be a really good screwdriver. And if, in general, you use your tools in this way—scissors for pliers, screwdrivers for levers, chisels for screwdrivers—your toolbox will in time become a collection of misshapen metal.

Something like this happens with words. "Fantastic," "great," "unique," "terrific," "tremendous" have quite blunted edges today, meaning no more than "very good." What did each once mean? How many words do we need for "very"? Isn't it a bit sad that sharp-edged chisel-like words like "awfully" and "terribly" are now just synonyms for "very"?

If Humpty Dumpty wants a word that means a nice knock-down argument, there's nothing to stop him from inventing one. He doesn't need "glory." He could call it, say, "garofash." "Garofash" has two advantages over "glory." In the first place it allows "glory" to go on meaning glory. There really isn't another good word for glory, so why blunt its edge? In the second place, if he said, "There's garofash for you!" you'd *have* to ask him what he meant by "garofash"; you couldn't assume that you knew.

Still, this is not so bad. The language changes and grows, and no one is really confused into thinking that a "cool" outfit is one designed to be worn on a hot summer day. Of course it can be both groovy and smooth. It's when people make words like "democracy" and "freedom" mean whatever they want them to mean that the real problems arise. Because how often is the listener going to stop and ask "What do you mean by democracy?"? He assumes he knows. Have you noticed that in the last twenty years or so *all* wars are defensive, no matter who fights them where? And how could it be otherwise for the United States, which dismissed its last Secretary of War from the President's cabinet over twenty years ago. Now we have only a Secretary of Defense. Now *there's* glory for you!

IX

Sounds, Noises, and Confusions

☐

"Him and I useta git along good, but now he don't like me no more."

How do you react to that sentence?

Do you have any trouble understanding it? If language is for the communication of information and ideas, why is there anything wrong with the sentence? Language must have other functions beyond communication.

Keen listeners can learn a great deal about speakers not just by what they say but by how they say it—their grammar, their choice of words, their accent. You can tell from the opening sentence that not only is the speaker uneducated but so also are her parents, so also are her friends. Do you think you know something about her "class"—not in school but in society? Is she of upper- or middle-class or lower-class background?

In England class distinctions can be discovered even more readily. The cockney who drops his h's or adds them in the wrong places is a familiar character, easy to spot, and the pattern of English working-class speech, which you may have heard in British movies, is so different from upper-class English and from standard American speech as to sound like a different language. Middle-class speech may be harder to distinguish from upper-class speech, but some amusing research has been done by Nancy Mitford and others on the differences between "U" and "non-U" English. ("U" stands for upper-class and "non-U" for everyone else.) Only part of the distinction is one of pronunciation. More often it is the choice of words themselves. "U" people "get sick" while the "non-U" are "ill." The "non-U" folk have "a lovely home" but the "U" live in "a very nice house." Non-U's look into "mirrors," U's into "looking-glasses." U's have "false teeth" but non-U's have "dentures."

Similar research in the city of Philadelphia found that upper-class people "washed" their clothes while the middle class "laundered" them. Upper-class people were "rich"; the moneyed middle class was "wealthy."

Do you put your groceries in a "bag" or a "sack"? Do you "tote" them home or do you "carry" them? If your friend is late, are you "waiting for" him or are you "waiting on" him? Perhaps you're worried about what has delayed him so that, later on, when you're telling the story of your afternoon, you'll say, "Was I ever glad to see him when he finally arrived!"

Do you call your mother's sister your "ont" or your "ant"? Are your eyebrows at the base of your "far-ed" or your "fore-hed"? Do you eat "ar-anges" or "or-anges," "tuh-may-toes" or "toe-mah-toes" or "tuh-may-ters"? If you said, "It would be merry to marry Mary," would someone listening be able to tell the three m-words apart? How about "That shot fell short of the target"?

The answers to all of the questions in the last two paragraphs depend on what part of the United States you were brought up in—both the choice of words and the pronunciation of those words that are common to all sections of the country.

If you compare British and American speech, the gaps are wider on both counts. Do you lift the "hood" or the "bonnet" to check the oil in your "lorry" or "truck"? Does it run on "gas" or on "petrol"? Are you buying it on "the installment plan" or "the hire-purchase plan"? Is is "lousy" or "bloody awful"?

A foreign accent, an unfamiliarity with the patterns of local speech, easily set the stranger apart from the community. In war time, if the speaker is in fact an ally but sounds like the enemy, he will need to know the passwords in order to survive.

Any word whatever can be a password. If you know the right sounds to make, the door will open as it did for Ali Baba with his magic words "open sesame." Passwords have their uses not only for military purposes but also for secret societies and, indeed, for any situation where it is important to discover rapidly and easily who are members of the "in" group. When doctors get together, or lawyers, or sailors, or skiers, or any group of people who share a trade, a profession, a hobby, a membership in a society, they are bound to use words that outsiders will not readily understand.

Can you discuss with a cook how to size up a chicken, how to draw it, how to try out the fat in a spider, and the fine points of dressing the chicken? What's the difference between the basting done by a cook and that done by a woman who's sewing?

Knowing the words to the right group of songs puts you in with the group, whether the song is "Clementine," "For Auld Lang Syne," or "The Star-Spangled Banner."

(Step aside for a moment for a footnote: Think about the words of "The Star Spangled Banner." Is it truly an appropriate message for the United States to present to the world today? Is "bombs bursting in air" our best image?) Is it the words of "The Star-Spangled Banner" that are important, or the participation in a ceremony of respect to flag and country? How old were you before you attached *any* meaning to the phrase " 'tis of thee" in the song "America"? "I pledge a legions to the flag of the United States of America and to the republicans for which it stands. One nation, under God, invisible, with liberty and just as for all" was one sixth-grader's version of the pledge. The sounds are right, the spirit of loyalty to flag and country are no less sincere than that of the boy next to him who can spell and pronounce the words correctly. What about responses in religious services when they are made in a language the congregation does not understand? Here again the words are used not for their meaning but for the feeling of uniting with a group in a ceremony of importance to all who are present.

Even more dependent on sound, less concerned with meaning and all involved with group emotion are cheers at games and pep rallies. Cheers have to be loud, should rhyme, and have a strong rhythm and should sound encouraging. Beyond that, it hardly matters what the words are. Hisses and boos, the imprecations of witches and the curses and name-calling of rowdies are more of the same. "Double, double, toil, and trouble" has no more meaning—and no less—than some of its unprintable modern equivalents. Are they all, in Shakespeare's words, "Full of sound and fury, signifying nothing"? The significance is there, but it is one of feeling, not of word meaning.

There's another aspect to cheers and curses, songs and pledges and prayers. They're like poems, and many poems, if not most, are written not to convey information but to evoke a feeling. A poem does not necessarily "mean" anything in the sense of having a readily available translation into ordinary English. When someone asked an abstract artist what his egg-shaped sculpture was supposed to be, he said, "A sculpture"—a perfectly sensible response.

Some poems depend almost entirely on the sound of words to create a mood in the listener. Any attempt at word-for-word or even phrase-for-phrase translation is likely to fail. The English poet of the early part of this century, Gerard Manley Hopkins, was the forerunner of many poets who use words in this way. This is the first stanza from his poem "Morning, Midday and Evening Sacrifice":

> The dappled die-away
> Cheek and wimpled lip,
> The gold-wisp, the airy-grey
> Eye, all in fellowship—
> This, all beauty blooming,
> This, all this freshness fuming,
> Give God while worth consuming.

The poetry of Dylan Thomas owes much to Hopkins, and many of his poems, like those of Hopkins, are concerned more with the music of words than with their definitions. What is such a poem supposed to mean? It means a poem.

The most common noninformational use of language is in the polite noises people make when they first meet.

"How do you do?" "Pleased to meet you," "Lovely weather we're having." There is a remarkable book by Desmond Morris, *The Naked Ape,* in which he studies human beings and discusses them as if he were a zoologist explaining the patterns of behavior of chimpanzees. Morris compares small talk about the weather to the "social grooming" that apes perform. If two apes wish to become friends, they do so by grooming each other over and over, even if the fur doesn't need grooming at all. The purpose is to allow the two to be together in a socially accepted activity and, by cooperating, to show that neither has any hostile intent. The human custom of offering a handshake as a means of greeting probably commenced as a gesture of real meaning: holding out one's right hand, the hand that *could* wield a sword or a knife, and showing it to be empty of weapons, offered a guarantee that no harm was intended. It was an invitation, therefore, to friendship.

Until a stranger speaks, you have no way of knowing whether he threatens you. Perhaps he is going to say "This is a stick-up." If you are closely confined with a stranger, in a small elevator, for example, you might find the situation frightening. Or perhaps the stranger might be frightened of you. Instead of the offered handshake, one of you is likely to say, for just the same effect, "Lovely weather we're having." A very large part of the words we speak every day are of this kind. They serve to break, and keep broken, a silence that might be regarded as unfriendly. What is said need not have meaning. It is a handshake.

In all of the uses of language so far discussed in this chapter, the meaning of the words is subordinate to the idea or association that the sounds of the words arouse.

In some, it does not matter if the words are without meaning. Language in these is a form of music. Some uses of language are at the opposite end of the stick: The words seem to be full of high significance and deep portent. Indeed they are so heavily loaded with meaning that the language fails to communicate because it is so obscure. Some public speeches are of this kind, loaded with high-sounding phrases, which, when analysed, boil down to nothing. Legal language and official government writing seems almost to be designed to confuse rather than to convey information. What is the advantage of saying the same thing three times or more as so many standard legal phrases do? "I do hereby make, publish and declare this to be my last will and testament" or "give, grant, bargain, sell and convey a certain tract of land, releasing all right, title, interest, claim and demand whatsoever"?

Suppose people generally spoke in this way? Can you translate the following school notice written in this style?

In full consideration of and giving due regard to the inclemency of the immediate and proximate atmospheric conditions in the locale and vicinity of this educational institution, the time span or interval normally and customarily devoted and consigned to outdoor physical activities and recreational pursuits will necessarily be curtailed.

At times the language of lawyers and doctors is so obscure that it might be considered a secret code. Possibly this is intended. The incantations of the witch doctors were carefully guarded secrets because if just *anyone* knew the words, the witch doctors might be out of a job. Wouldn't today's pharmacist understand the doctor's note if he wrote "12 tablets of penicillin, 50 units each" instead of the seemingly illegible prescription he does write? Wouldn't the judge understand the lawyer just as well if he said "buyer" and "seller" instead of "party of the first part" and "party of the second part"? Yes, but so would you. And then some of the wizardry would be lost. You might feel that you could buy your own medicine, write your own contract. You might even feel cheated if your lawyer drew up a will for you in simple, straightforward English, all of which you could understand. What was he being paid for, after all? It's his job to write "I give, devise, and bequeath." If all it takes, is "I give," you could write it yourself.

Some language is unquestionably designed to confuse. Suppose what you have to say isn't too likely to be accepted heartily. Can you dress it up in words that make your point more glamorous and attractive? A fairly subtle way of insuring that your listener hears what you want him to hear and reacts as you wish him to is to cast your sentence in a form that looks logically self-evident. This sign, some version of which appears in many small stores, is a fine example:

WE HAVE AN AGREEMENT WITH OUR BANK.
THEY DON'T REPAIR SHOES AND WE DON'T CASH CHECKS.

For "We don't cash checks," substitute "We don't make change" or "We don't handle money." The sign won't be quite so persuasive.

Would you fall for the trick in this ad?

Fresh eggs or dried eggs?
A cake like this? Fresh eggs, of
course. That's why Betty Crocker says,
"*You add the eggs* to my cake mixes.
You know *the eggs are fresh.*"
Unlike most cake mixes, there are
NO DRIED EGG WHITES, NO DRIED EGG
YOLKS, NO DRIED EGGS OF ANY KIND IN
BETTY CROCKER
CAKE MIXES

Do you want fresh milk in your cake, too? Whole chocolate? Real butter? Then you'd better not buy a cake mix. But if you're going to buy one, why buy the one that offers *less* than the others?

"Acoustical know-how has been poorly communicated," said a recent television speaker. "Few Railroad engineers even know how to spell acoustics." Shocking! Compare: "My baby brother is so selfish he doesn't even know how to spell generosity." Are there, perhaps, some devoted toxophilites who never even heard of the word?

The simplest form of using language to confuse rather than to inform is in the choice of a name that will arouse all the hoped-for association. Duz does everything. All does too. And if you want to sell perfume to a man who ordinarily regards perfume as feminine, you'd better call it Hai Karate or Brut. The neatest example of this use of language was in the naming of a town in Japan. Before World War II cheap Japanese toys and gadgets flooded the United States, and people were leery of goods marked "Made in Japan" because they tended to fall apart rather quickly. A Japanese town named Usa solved the importers' problem for a while. Goods produced there could be stamped "MADE IN USA."

Language is for the communication of information and ideas. Yes, but . . . it is also for cooing and growling and barking and yelping and purring. It is also for saying, by the sound of the words alone, who you are, where you're from, what sort of person you are. It is also for covering a thought with a blanket of words so thick you can't see through them. Sometimes, instead of asking, "What does it mean?" ask first, "Was it supposed to mean something?"

Now that's a fine note on which to end a book about language. We've told you everything once and some things twice. We won't tell you anything three times, because truth just isn't that easy to come by.

A Note on Sources

You may remember the story of the son of an electrical engineer who asked his mother to explain how a flashlight worked. When she asked him why he didn't go to his father, he said, "Because I don't want to know *that* much about it."

It would be pleasant to say, "If you have enjoyed this book and would like to read more like it, here is a list of related books." Unfortunately, for the present, this isn't possible. Much has been written in the field of semantics and linguistics, but, except for a recent book by Stuart Chasen, *Danger—Men Talking* (Parents' Magazine Press, 1969), none of it is written for young readers. Nevertheless, it would not be quite fair to pretend that all of the ideas in this book are original nor to deprive you of the chance of delving deeper into any particular aspect of the subject of semantics you might want to pursue. Therefore, here is a brief list of some of the books that have been useful in the writing of this book. If you do want to know *"that* much" about the subject, you might try some of them.

The best general book you can find about how language affects thinking and behavior is S. I. Hayakawa's *Language in Thought and Action* (Harcourt Brace and Company, 1949), a book you will undoubtedly meet in some college course. Other general books are Irving J. Lee's *Language Habits in Human Affairs* (Harper & Brothers, 1941) and Wendell Johnson's *People in Quandaries* (Harper & Brothers, 1946).

To follow further the question of the relation between language and prejudice, as discussed in Chapter I, you might delve into *The Nature of Prejudice* by Gordon W. Allport (Anchor Books, 1958).

Anyone who writes of the differences between the Hopi and the English-American languages is dependent upon the research and writing of Benjamin Lee Whorf. Much of Chapter V is based on articles by Whorf and by Anatol Rapaport, collected in *Language, Meaning and Maturity*, edited by S. I. Hayakawa (Harper & Brothers, 1954). The information about the Navajo language comes from *The Navaho* by Clyde Kluckhohn and Dorothea Leighton (Harvard University Press, 1951), a book that will tell you a great deal about the Navajo's customs, religion, and ways of life as well as their language.

On the subject of taboos and euphemisms, discussed in Chapter VI, there is a great deal of fascinating material to be found in Isaac Goldberg's *The Wonder of Words* (D. Appleton-Century Company, 1939), in Margaret Schlauch's *The Gift of Language* (Dover Publications, 1955), and in Dwight Bolinger's *Aspects of Language* (Harcourt, Brace and World, Inc., 1968).

Other books which have been helpful in the writing of this book, but which you would probably find rather rough going, are Benjamin Lee Whorf's *Language, Thought and Reality* (The Technology Press of M.I.T. and John Wiley and Sons, Inc., 1956) ; A *Study of Thinking* by Jerome S. Bruner and others (John Wiley and Sons, Inc., 1957); Max Wertheimer's *Productive Thinking* (Harper & Brothers, 1945) ; and Roger Brown's *Words and Things* (Free Press of Glencoe, 1958) .

Index